THE MEDIEVAL
BOY BISHOPS

THE MEDIEVAL
BOY BISHOPS

NEIL MACKENZIE

Matador
9 Priory Business Park
Kibworth Beauchamp
Leicestershire LE8 0RX, UK
Tel: (+44) 116 279 2299
Fax: (+44) 116 279 2277
Email: books@troubador.co.uk
Web: www.troubador.co.uk/matador

ISBN 978 1780880 082

British Library Cataloguing in Publication Data.
A catalogue record for this book is available from the British Library.

Typeset in Adobe Garamond Pro by Troubador Publishing Ltd, Leicester, UK
Printed and bound in the UK by TJ International, Padstow, Cornwall

Matador is an imprint of Troubador Publishing Ltd

To my mother and father to whom I owe just about everything.

The past is a foreign country: they do things differently there.

The Go Between – L P Hartley

Acknowledgements

I should like to thank Richard Urquhart, Jeremy Eyre, Stephen Holland, Elizabeth Burke, Kora Jones, Hélène Gargett and my sister, Rosemary Ryan, for their invaluable help with translation.

My thanks are also due to Robert Layton and Michael Barcroft for their patience and advice.

Any defects and errors are mine.

Cover illustration: The Boy Bishop, Benjamin Odell, enthroned at All Saints' Cathedral, Albany, NY, in 1992.

I am grateful to Daniel Odell for permission to use this photograph.

Introduction

An accident of history

It was a mistake that first led to the rediscovery of the Boy Bishop ceremonies.

In the first half of the seventeenth century in Salisbury Cathedral when some seats under the pulpit were removed by workmen during renovations, a small marble effigy, some 86cm in length, of a bishop in full robes, was uncovered, as Canon John Gregory relates:

> *...in the cathedral of Sarum there lieth a monument in stone, of a little boie habited all in episcopal robes, a miter upon his head, a crosier in his hand and the rest accordingly. The monument lay long buried under the seats near the pulpit, at the removal whereof it was of late years discovered...*[1]

Gregory was puzzled by this find since it seemed impossible that an adult bishop could be of so small a stature, or that a boy's tomb should be surmounted by the effigy of a bishop. Accordingly, when he ventured to find the solution, he discovered the statute of Roger de Mortival *De Episcopo Choristarum* (Concerning the Bishop of the Choristers) which *"plainly appeareth"* to show that the effigy represented a Boy Bishop who had died in office. Further research uncovered the form of the Boy Bishop's liturgy in the *Sarum Processionale* and so began the study of the Boy Bishop.

Yet Gregory had made an uncharacteristic blunder for such a careful scholar. He had made a link between the effigy and the Boy Bishop ceremonies relying solely on his intuition, but unwarranted by evidence. In fact, a little more consideration of the effigy itself would have revealed to Gregory that at 86cm it could hardly represent the size of a Boy Bishop. It is closer to the height of a child of about two years old. The likelihood is that beneath the effigy lay buried only the heart or other internal organs of a true bishop, the rest of his body resting elsewhere, or that the sculpture was crafted in this way according to a will, the wishes of his family, or the whim of the sculptor.[2]

The Salisbury effigy, which was moved to its current location on the south side of the nave, is now thought to commemorate Richard Poore, bishop from 1217 to 1228, who planned and oversaw the construction of the present cathedral. However, it is not entirely inappropriate that his effigy has been considered to be that of a Boy Bishop, the representative of the boys, for in his time at Salisbury their welfare was close to his heart. He tried to improve their education by instituting a monitorial system: the clergy were to instruct some of the boys in doctrine and prayers, and they in turn were to instruct others. He gave some schoolmasters benefices on the condition that they did not charge for their teaching, and he also instructed his clergy to preach every Sunday that children should not be left alone in the home with fire or water. It is believed that his heart was buried under his effigy, while the rest of his body most likely lies in Tarrant Crawford Abbey in accordance with his wishes.

Others, following Gregory's error, also misattributed effigies; for instance, a sculpture of a figure of just over half a metre in length at Bindon was at one time mistakenly believed to be that of a Boy Abbot. St Oswald's church in Filey is said to have, on the south wall of the nave, a carved figure of a Boy Bishop who died in office between 1250 and 1300, although some maintain that it is the memorial to a member of the laity whose heart is buried there.

There were violent deaths associated with ceremonies in Salisbury, St Petersburg, Ratisbon and of Bartholomew Divitis in Paris, but there was also a sad case where the Boy Bishop died during his tenure and was given a memorial. In Lille it seems that the Boy Bishop continued to represent the choirboys at certain festivities during the year.[3] The Boy Bishop of 1500/1501, Guillemot de Lespine, died on 29th June 1501 of natural causes and received his burial in the cloister, the honour of its location perhaps having more to do with the high status of his mother Agnes Bordebecq than with the status accorded to the boy's office.

John Gregory, who believed that the Boy Bishop was unique to Salisbury, would have probably been surprised, and perhaps gratified, that, despite his error, his initial inquiries have led to the uncovering of so much material by scholars across Europe.

The materials and approach

The starting points for any serious study of the Boy Bishop are the detailed accounts given in *The Medieval Stage* by E K Chambers and in both parts of C H

Evelyn-White's *The Boy Bishop* (Episcopus Puerorum) *of Mediaeval England.* This book is an attempt to build on those foundations, drawing on material not available to either author and considering the wider perspective in order to produce a comprehensive study, presenting as far as possible all the important features and variations.

Any writer on the subject owes a huge debt to those nineteenth and early twentieth century scholars who unearthed a wealth of material from many varied sources. Although most of the evidence for the Boy Bishop comes from England, France and Spain, there are sources which provide information from across western Europe and beyond. We are lucky to possess detailed records from a number of churches, cathedrals and religious houses, but from many others there are just fleeting references giving mere glimpses into the ceremonies.

Perhaps the greatest surprise to those studying the Boy Bishop is that, in England at least, he was so quickly forgotten. That such important, vibrant, colourful ceremonies which provided one of the most impressive focuses of the Christmas season could have faded from the national memory in less than a century after their final suppression is perhaps an indication of how quickly and ruthlessly the new Protestantism erased the memory of the Old Religion.

Any history of the Boy Bishop should perhaps take account of four different ways of relating his story. There is, first of all, the broad narrative across the centuries, which deals with his origins, continuance throughout the Middle Ages, suppression and revival. Although this provides a secure enough framework, reliance on this approach alone must of necessity exclude most of what is interesting in the study, for either one would have to rely on broad generalisations or to relate the story from the narrow perspective of one cathedral alone. There is also a need to engage with the closer chronology of the ceremonies and to discover what happened in the annual cycle, from the Boy Bishop's election to the end of his tenure. Moreover, a full account requires an examination of parallel examples from different towns, cities, schools and religious houses. Finally, there are the historical by-ways offered by the stories of some of the individuals who played their own parts in the history.

It is to be hoped that the breadth and detail of this study, which aims to present the Boy Bishop's place in history and to give some insight into one aspect of the medieval period with its celebrations and tensions, glories and dark shadows, will more than compensate for a failure to concentrate solely on the forward movement of the historical narrative.

The monument in Salisbury Cathedral that John Gregory mistakenly believed to be a tomb of a Boy Bishop

1

The Murder of a Boy Bishop

On the morning of 7th December 1367 the body of a boy floated unnoticed down the River Seine away from Paris. Even had they noticed the corpse, it is unlikely that in general the people of Paris would have raised little more than a murmur of sympathy, given that violence of all sorts was an element of that restless and colourful city life, were it not for one remarkable fact: the boy was dressed in the authentic robes of a bishop. It was these robes that would have immediately identified him as the principal participant in an ancient, popular and highly revered religious rite, a rite celebrated across most of Western Europe in churches and cathedrals, priories and abbeys, schools and universities, a rite that for all its vigour, controversy, importance and beauty is now generally forgotten.

The complete story stretches across many centuries, perhaps as far back as the Romans and certainly as far forward as the present day. Part of the story is how and why the boy came to be murdered and what happened afterwards. But it is also the story of how he came to be wearing bishop's robes, a stranger and more interesting tale altogether.

The corpse was the body of the Boy Bishop.[1] His name was Bartholomew Divitis.

Although there had been at least one attempt to end it, by 1367 the custom of the Parisian students electing one of their number as Boy Bishop was well-established, as was the subsequent torch-lit procession through the Parisian streets, with the Boy adorned in episcopal robes and regalia, to the house of a university rector and to the houses of other masters and students.[2]

The dead Boy had been elected in the house of Peter de Zippa on the evening before St Nicholas's Day, 6th December, a significant date in the broader story. Peter de Zippa was a well-known and apparently respected figure who had himself once been a rector of the university. Now he was a master, his scholars boarding with him in his house, as was the practice. However, he had come into conflict with the watch on a previous occasion. It seems that on the vigil of St Catherine's Day the watch had surrounded his house, seized him, beaten him, and taken him to prison. However, the Préfet having found the charges to be against reason and justice, condemned them and released him. The consequences of this were to be disastrous and fatal. The watch had not forgotten their previous humiliation and they craved revenge.

The scholars, with their Boy Bishop, Bartholomew Divitis, dressed in bishop's robes, set out from Peter de Zippa's house their voices echoing in the dark Paris streets as they made their way in the flickering yellow light of the torches, youngsters seeking fun in the gloomy, cold months of winter. No doubt they were noisy, high-spirited and raucous in the manner of young men throughout the ages but they were completely unarmed, intending no harm to anyone. Many would be destined for the priesthood – some were already ordained into the order of subdeacon – and occasions such as these provided a chance for lighter amusement before the heavier responsibilities of the priestly life.

Having made their visitation to the rector, they allowed the youngest members of the group to lead the way back, but it was their misfortune to meet four members of the watch who took their chance and immediately attacked these leading members of the unarmed group with drawn swords, seriously injuring James de Buissono in the leg. Naturally, the older scholars rushed to their aid, but being unarmed could only explain to the watch as calmly as possible that this attack was completely unwarranted. Their explanation simply seemed to inflame matters and one of the watch became so enraged that it required his three companions to restrain him in his murderous fury. Perhaps the watch had lain in wait for them; perhaps it was merely an unlucky encounter. But, whatever the truth, from this point events moved quickly and the violence veered out of control.

With the commotion thus created, other members of the watch, on foot and on horseback, hurried to the scene, including the officer of the watch, Philip de Villaribus, and Bernard Blondelli, his lieutenant. They drew their swords and, with the loud and fearful cry of "To the death", they charged. The terrified scholars fled. Having reached home with the injured boy, they barricaded all the entrances to the house. The watch was not to be so easily discouraged. After hurling insults at the retreating scholars, they began to attack the house with a hail of stones, and arrows sent from bows and ballistas; more the fury of an attack on an enemy force, it was reported, than the watch going about its business.

Peter de Zippa clearly understood the peril in which he and his companions stood, so he stepped up to an open window to negotiate with the attackers. The watch, in no mood for negotiation, continued to fire at the house. Peter was wounded in the chest. Three inches to the side, this wound would have been fatal. Another was hit in the arm with an arrow. The watch tried to persuade them to surrender shouting at them in Latin and French so that – it was claimed – all might understand. In the manner of those who feel that they wield unaccountable power, they offered "protection" if the defenders would give themselves up but threat of harm and injury if they did not.

Whether in anger at the unjustified violence of the watch, or from desperate bravado, those inside the house began to shout defiance at the besiegers and to throw stones and logs out of the windows. One large stone hit a horse injuring it; another hit Peter Patou smashing four of his teeth. For a while it seemed as though he were dead, but he was merely knocked unconscious. Philip de Vallaribus was wounded in the shin, but having his head unprotected was lucky to have escaped worse injury.

It became obvious to the watch that if they wanted arrests and their revenge they would have to adopt a different strategy. They called for blacksmiths' hammers and began to smash their way into the building. Those inside made a last, desperate attempt to resist by defending the breech with swords and lances, but it was to no avail. Peter de Zippa, seeing that they would be unable to continue their resistance, surrendered. The watch entered the house in the manner of thugs, smashing and looting. Neither were they any more gentle with Peter and his companions. Having seized them violently, they threw one of the youngsters down some steps from which he received a number of head wounds. He recovered somewhat and in fear of his life fled towards the River Seine with members of the watch in close pursuit. When he reached the river he was faced with re-capture and no doubt a beating and worse, or a suicidal jump into the dark water. He jumped. Luck was on his side for the first time that night. He was hauled out by a woman who just happened to be in the right place.

Meanwhile the others had been beaten, rounded up and made to sit in the filth of the street. Here they were viciously assaulted with a vehemence usually reserved for robbers or enemy soldiers. Then they were seized roughly and marched to the Castle prison accompanied by more blows and insults. Meanwhile, the soldiers tried to drown another scholar, John Crampe, in the Seine, but he put up a good fight and successfully resisted the attempt. The twenty-five who were brought to the Castle were thrown into the stinking, dark prison with one bed between them all. And there they remained that night.

The violence of that night was shocking enough, but tragedy was to follow. Nobody could find Bartholomew Divitis, the Boy Bishop himself. The scholars remembered that he had been in their company as they made their visitation to the Rector and even until the time that they had met the watch. After the attack in the street, things had become far less clear. Nobody remembered seeing him after that. It seemed that, separated from the others, he had been caught by the watch, murdered and his body thrown into the Seine. No subsequent searches ever found it.

After a complaint was brought, the *Parlement* commissioned an enquiry. To justify their vengeful, hot-headed violence, the watch presented their attack as an act of self-defence, relying on the injuries they had sustained and on the actions of Peter de Zippa and his companions in defending the house. It was a feeble enough excuse and not deemed sufficient justification, so further enquiries were made, which included the use of torture. The truth finally emerged and those of the watch who had participated in the violence were sentenced to imprisonment and payment of damages. In addition, they were ordered to make a humiliating public apology with bare heads, on their knees to the Bishop of Paris, the Rector, Peter de Zippa and his scholars in the cloister or chapter house of the church of St Mathurin.

There is an unpleasant parallel to this story in Salisbury. [3] At 8 o'clock on the evening of 27th December, 1448 the choristers made their way back to their lodging house after an evening of celebration at the house of a canon. As they went they presented an unruly spectacle which was made worse by the behaviour of a group of vicars who went with them. There was a fracas and for some reason the boys began attacking the vicars with sticks. A particular argument broke out between one of the vicars and a retainer of the canon at whose house the boys had been entertained and who had been sent to accompany them home. It is not clear whether he was sent to protect the boys from the undesirables who lurked in the cathedral grounds, or to protect others from the boys. The argument continued to the choristers' residence where, in the ensuing fight, the retainer was murdered by the vicar.

There was an enquiry. As a result much scandalous behaviour was brought to light. It seems that the vicars who sang and read in the cathedral services as part of the Boy Bishop celebrations had been accustomed to use *"howling and profanity"* and to mock the religious nature of the feast. Things had been broken, silk copes (vestments of great value) had been damaged and candles had been stolen. The *Statute for restraining the insolence of the choristers* aimed to put an end to these abuses. The vicars were strictly forbidden to carry offensive weapons unless they were attending Matins in the dark, or setting out or returning from a journey to distant parts, on the sensible grounds that the carrying of such weapons more often than not merely encouraged the bearers to commit acts of violence rather than simply being a means of defence. The choristers too, if they wished to continue their customs, were to make their way to and from the Christmas celebrations without carrying sticks or making a noise. All this presents a glimpse of the rowdy and somewhat threatening atmosphere after dark in the Cathedral Close.

In 1137 the chronicle of the monastery of St Petersburg near Halle mentions that during the Boy Bishop ceremonies a boy had been trodden to death.[4] There was also a murder in Ratisbon in 1357.[5]

Children's celebrations and appalling violence seem to make unpalatable companions. But this was an age of excesses.

> *So violent and motley was life that it bore the mixed smell of blood and roses. The men of that time always oscillate between the fear of hell and the most naïve joy, between cruelty and tenderness, between harsh asceticism and insane attachments to the joys of this world, between hatred and goodness, always running to extremes.* [6]

The disorder and violence engendered by these celebrations existed alongside their religious nature, and the Church as a whole not only countenanced them but was prepared to give them official sanction and to provide a full ecclesiastical framework for them.

The Church's attitude might appear to be somewhat strange, yet the key to understanding it lies in the origin of the ceremonies, in the ceremonies themselves and in the patterns of medieval thought.

The Origins of the Boy Bishop

It is not possible to identify with any accuracy the origins of the Boy Bishop ceremonies. We cannot say with any confidence that they began in a particular place on a particular date, partly because they seem to have developed slowly over many years and partly because early medieval records are incomplete. There are, however, a number of influences that could have contributed to their institution.

The long winter months would have seemed bleaker, darker and colder to those living in Europe in the Middle Ages than they do to us today. While most of us enjoy the benefits of heating, lighting, readily available transport and a wide variety of food, even fruits and vegetables which are out of season, to those in a medieval town or village winter life presented a radically different reality.[1] Heating in houses was rudimentary and inefficient; for most houses were heated by a central fire, the smoke escaping through the thatch or the eaves; and there was no escaping the draughts. Even during daylight hours houses would be dark. There being no glass (an exceedingly expensive luxury beyond the means of most) in the windows, these would be shuttered against the cold. There was little to do when darkness fell. What light there was would be provided by the glow of fire or, if they could be afforded, tallow dips or candles. The restricted diet of the majority of the population would be limited even further in the winter months. For many in England, for example, bread and potage made from peas, oats or leeks, and perhaps containing herbs, meat stock, beans and a little bacon would constitute the staple diet, with comparatively few extras to be added. Winter was a time when there were few fresh vegetables available except those that could be successfully stored. Wealthier people could afford a better and more varied diet, but even for them the season reduced choice. Travelling, always a problem in this period, was even more difficult in winter. The days were short and it was important to reach a town before the gates closed for the night. Roads, rutted and uneven in the summer, might become muddy quagmires in winter. In most towns it would have been fairly hazardous to venture out into the unlit streets at night for fear of robbers waiting in the shadows, and a curfew might have prevented this anyway. Curfews were commonplace: the town gates would be shut, taverns would close and permission to wander the streets would be granted to relatively few.

Given the gloom and misery of a medieval winter it is hardly surprising that people sought ways in which to find cheer and solace. For medieval people most forms of recreation and amusement were communal and so it can be no surprise that religious celebrations and feasting feature prominently in this season. The bright fires of celebration might help to hold at bay the winter shadows and the cold. The most obvious time for celebration was Christmas Day, but this was by no means the only day. Among others there were the Feast of Fools, actually three feasts held on 26th December, 27th December and 1st January, a fascinating study in itself, and the ceremonies of the Boy Bishop. The festivities attendant on the election and period in office of the Boy Bishop not only offered a glorious religious celebration with the added *frisson* of seeing senior clerics replaced and humbled, but they also presented opportunities for processions, drinking, eating and generally making merry, as well as the chance for more unbridled behaviour. It was as if the shackles of life had been loosened for a while.

The antecedents for the ceremonies as they developed later may well lie in the abbey at St Gall, one of the most important and influential Benedictine abbeys, the song school of which was instrumental in developing the music and ceremonial of the Church.[2] Perhaps, because of the emphasis placed on education and music, the boys were allotted their own special celebration which included a highly impressive Vespers procession, in line with those given to the deacons and priests. The fame of these processions spread widely, coming to the notice of King Conrad I in the happier days early in his reign, before he faced his unsuccessful struggles to establish his kingship against powerful dukes. Thus in 911, during the Christmas season, Conrad, who was staying with Bishop Solomon of Constance, determined to visit the abbey at St Gall to witness the famed processions.

He clearly enjoyed the experience, so much so that he determined to add to it himself. He seems to have retained some boyish impishness, and planned something unexpected for the choristers. As darkness fell on the Feast of Holy Innocents the great abbey church was prepared for Vespers, one of the most important of the monastic offices, given greater significance because of the great procession of choristers. Numbers of candles had been lit casting the altar in a warm yellow glow and softening the shadows in the corners. The highly dignified procession of the choristers began and Conrad's plan was executed. His followers began rolling apples along the aisle in hope that the sight of this sought-after fruit would prove too much of a temptation for the boys and they would break ranks in pursuit of it. However, the choristers had been well-trained (or were perhaps fearful of the wrath to come if they marred the dignity of the procession) and Conrad was left marvelling that not only did not one of the choristers, not even the smallest, stretch out a hand for an apple but that they were all completely unmoved by his stunt, possibly even contemptuous of the attempt. A music book of Winchester Cathedral shows that by 979 the choristers were accorded a position of some importance on the Feast of Holy Innocents. They were given a hymn containing the words: *Hymn ye now Christ, ye boys, in the words of the prophet, Domine, Dominus.*[3]

There is evidence of a Boy Bishop at Rouen in the early part of the tenth century[4] and Beletus notes that the ceremonies were established in Europe by 1182, with bishops and archbishops often taking part in the festivities with their inferiors. He, however, criticises as demeaning this behaviour that sometimes went as far as playing ball games.[5]

It is just possible that the Boy Bishop in the Greek Church predates his western counterpart. Cedranus relates that about the year 990 Theophylact, the Patriarch of Constantinople, instituted the election of a pseudo-bishop together with the associated festivities.[6] There is some doubt, however, whether he was in truth a Boy Bishop or a bishop in the tradition of the more unruly Feast of Fools.[7]

Perhaps a key date in establishing the origins of the Boy Bishop ceremonies is May 1087 when the relics of St Nicholas were translated from Myra in Lycia to Bari in Italy, although "stolen" might be a more accurate description of what happened in this remarkable story. Not surprisingly, following the success of such a daring expedition, the cult of St Nicholas spread across Europe. The growth in his popularity was aided by many legends which had grown up around him. Two of the most famous concern children. In one he is said to have prevented a poor father from selling his three daughters into slavery for want of dowries by throwing bags of gold through the window on three separate occasions. The legend states that the bags of gold landed in stockings left to dry before the fire, so giving rise to our custom of leaving out stockings on Christmas Eve. On another occasion, an Asian father, in order to educate his three sons, sent them to Athens, where they were to wait on the bishop for his blessing. When they arrived in Myra they decided to delay their visit until the next day and sought lodgings at an inn, where the innkeeper murdered them, cut them up, salted them and put them in a barrel, in order to take possession of their belongings and to sell them as pork to unsuspecting customers. St Nicholas, the bishop, having been given a vision of the crime, made his way to the inn and accused the innkeeper of the dreadful deed. After his confession, the innkeeper begged for the bishop's prayers, and St Nicholas, believing in his contrition, prayed that he might be forgiven and for life to be restored to the boys. The prayer concluded, it was reported that the dismembered parts of the boys were reunited and the boys stood forth. After finally receiving the bishop's blessing they continued their journey to Athens to follow their studies. It is a pity that the boys themselves seem to have left no account of their sensational ordeal. It followed, therefore, that among those who were specifically placed under his protection were children. The growth of devotion to St Nicholas provided the opportunity to link the choristers' feast with a popular saint whose day fell conveniently in the winter period on 6th December.

Maybe, when establishing the foundations of the Boy Bishop ceremonies, those early churchmen remembered the ancient Roman feast of Saturnalia (although the Faculty of Theology in Paris saw their origins in celebrations in honour of Janus[8]). This was a time of giving gifts, a time when, for a day, the role of masters and slaves would be reversed and the masters would be expected to serve meals to their slaves who were also given the unaccustomed privileges of leisure and the chance to gamble. It was also a time when schoolboys would be given a holiday and a *Saturnalicius princeps* elected, a sort of Lord of Misrule who presided over the often raucous celebrations. The satirist Lucian has Saturn proclaim through his priest:

> *During my week the serious is barred; no business allowed. Drinking, noise and games and dice, appointing of kings and feasting of slaves, singing naked, clapping of frenzied hands, an occasional ducking in icy water of faces covered in burnt cork.*[9]

Many of the elements of the Roman feast can be found in the Boy Bishop celebrations, although it is not possible now to say for sure whether the Romans inspired the medieval churchmen in this way. Perhaps both feasts developed along similar lines because they answered people's needs in the harsh days of winter.

Another factor in the development of the ceremonies might have been the response of the medieval mind to threats present in the world. The dangers facing children were manifold. Illness was a constant shadow. With very limited understanding of how disease was transmitted, medieval parents were fairly powerless to protect their children from its ravages, and a comparative lack of sanitation made the threat worse. If it were not possible to breast-feed a baby (either by the mother herself or by an expensive wet-nurse), its chances of receiving contaminated milk would be increased significantly. Many children died after accidents in houses that were far less child-friendly than those of today, and in an outside world that was similarly full of hazards. One sad case may act as an illustration. In 1301, eight year old Richard le Mazon, having finished his dinner and returning to school thought that he would entertain himself, as boys are wont to do, by showing off his physical strength and agility as he crossed London Bridge.

> *...he hung by his hands in play from a certain beam on the side of the bridge, so that, his hands giving way, he fell into the water and was drowned* .[10]

Parents who were necessarily busy were often not able to give their young children proper supervision and they were constantly left unattended and subject to the assorted dangers of the age. Joan de Irlaunde, a baby one month old, lived in London in a rented shop with her parents. An hour before Vespers she was left in her cradle while her parents went out leaving her unattended, with the shop door open since it was mid-May and warm. While her parents were gone a pig wandered into the house and bit the right side of her head inflicting a mortal wound. She died later in her mother's arms. This occurred despite it being forbidden to allow pigs to wander the London streets.[11] In times of famine the young were among the most vulnerable members of society. It is estimated that 25% of babies died within their first year and that a further 20% died before reaching the age of twenty. Whether the affection that bound parent to child was as strong in this period as it is today is a matter for some conjecture but no doubt the mortality rate affected the outlook of the medieval mind, for parents had to be prepared to accept that there was a good chance that their offspring would not survive into adulthood. It might be going too far to insist that parents more-or-less disregarded their children as personalities until they reached the age of discretion, that childhood was in fact unimportant, but certainly they needed great stoicism in the face of death and there may well have lurked in the back of the mind the idea that a short life soon ended was not worthy of remembrance. It was thought necessary to have several children so that there was the likelihood that at least some would survive. With death an unseen, lurking presence, always close at hand, especially for the young, parents might well have been wary of investing too much emotional capital in something that might be snatched away.

To some degree at least society regarded children as dispensable and accordingly courts were reluctant to convict parents whose children had died as a result of their neglect – *"Nobody thought, as we ordinarily think today, that every child already contained a man's personality".*[12] There was some religious precedent for this view, for after all the Gospel writers themselves give no account of Christ's childhood, except for his birth and his disputing with the teachers in the temple when he was twelve. Even the Saviour's childhood did not seem worthy of record.

However, as the Middle Ages progressed, attitudes began to change and there was a growing understanding of the importance of children and childhood. This change was gradual and patchy but ultimately it has helped to form our understanding of the young. The Church had always taught that everyone, including the very young, had a soul. A recognition of how this teaching might be reflected in day-to-day attitudes began to develop. Vincent de Beauvais felt able to write in 1481:

> *the service rendered God in youth is more precious to him than that of old age for youth offers to God the best of life, the flower, the vigour...Boys have even natural virtues – virginity, innocence, humility...* (De Eruditione Principum, Book 5, chapter 5)

Children began to be given a more prominent place in medieval society and their true human value increasingly came to be recognised. The Boy Bishop ceremonies can be seen as both influencing and in turn reflecting this changing of perception.

The Wheel of Fortune is often depicted in medieval art with the human figures at the mercy of Fortune's caprice as she spins her wheel randomly. In an age when the proud, the powerful and successful could be toppled by the sudden workings of man or fate, the instability of worldly things was symbolised by a boy unseating a bishop in his own cathedral.

O Fortuna,
velut Luna
statu variabilis
semper crescis

aut decrescis;
vita detestabilis
nunc obdurat
et tunc curat
ludo mentis aciem;
egestatem
potestatem
dissolvit ut glaciem.

Sors immanis
et inanis
rota tu volubilis
status malus
vana salus
semper dissolubilis;
obumbrata
et velata
mihi quoque niteris;
nunc per ludem
dorsum nudum
fero tui sceleris.

Sors salutis
et virtutis
mihi nunc contraria;
est affectus
et defectus
semper in angaria.
hac in hora
sine mora
cordae pulsum tangite!
quod per sortem
sternit fortem
mecum omnes plangite!

from Carmina Burana

O Fortune just as the moon with a varying state you are always waxing or waning; hateful life now hard and next heals the power of the mind with a game; it melts poverty and power like ice.

Fate savage and foolish, you a turning wheel, stand malevolent, vain prosperity, always likely to disappear; shadowed and veiled you press upon me too; now through your sport of wickedness I bear a naked back.

The chance of prosperity and virtue hostile to me; it is moved and diminishes in slavery. In this hour without delay touch the beat of the string, because through Fate she destroys the strong. All mourn with me.

Even bishops could fall from favour and boys could aspire to the episcopal throne.

No doubt those clerics in charge of the boys' education in the choir schools and elsewhere played their part too in establishing the ceremonies. Education was a bleak and monotonous affair for many boys. Parents and schoolmasters alike were considered neglectful if they failed to discipline their children physically, and the medieval schoolmaster's motto was *quot verba, tot verbera* (with as many words as blows). The rod was used on the head and hands while the birch was applied to the backside. Holidays away from school were in all probability non-existent for most. There were holidays in the original sense of *holy days* but on these days the boys would be expected to attend the church, not only for Mass, but for other offices and processions too. Ball games were probably forbidden in most places. Like prison everywhere, the school walls must have crushed the spirits of many and stoked resentment in others. Some masters undoubtedly, who recalled their own school days and possessing not only sympathy but the courage and imagination to challenge the accepted constraints, would have sought legitimate recreational opportunities for their charges within this harsh system. The Boy Bishop ceremonies, with associated dressing up, feasting and visiting, would have provided one such opportunity.

Whatever the inspiration, by the late Middle Ages and the beginning of the Renaissance the Boy Bishop ceremonies had spread right across Western Europe and beyond, even as far as Peru.[13]

The Election of the Boy Bishop

Life was, at least by our standards, hard and demanding in the medieval choir schools and colleges, yet the Christmas season offered the prospect of welcome relief. Although Christmas Day itself would undoubtedly have been an important feast for these boys in the Middle Ages, featuring prominently in their religious understanding and, for some at least, holding deep religious significance, it is to be doubted that the age-long desire of boys for the enjoyments of eating, drinking, merry-making and mischief-making was lacking in these choristers and scholars. There might be no surviving accounts from this period written by the boys describing their Christmas season experiences, but it is not hard to surmise, given the accounts of what they got up to, that the election of the Boy Bishop with the attendant ceremonies, was, if not the highlight of the season, certainly one of the most anticipated events of the year. What made it so special in both religious and secular terms is described in later chapters, and strange reading it makes to those used to decorum and restraint in the Church's liturgy.

It is easy to interpret the Middle Ages through a twenty-first century perspective and to misunderstand it. Medieval man was both very like and very unlike us and the same applies to boys. In Britain in the eighteenth and nineteenth centuries, an age when Catholicism was widely regarded with a suspicion and even fear, many saw the ceremonies simply as "priest-craft", medieval mummery and farce.[1] But these were the objections of those sensitive to the slightest whiff of "popery". Actually, it is possible to identify, if not a mild anti-clericism, at least a check on the clergy in the election of the Boy Bishop and the ceremonies that followed. In fact, in the election of the Boy Bishop the choristers were given much freedom and responsibility, at least in most places, although there were attempts to curtail this. There was indeed much to look forward to here for the medieval cathedral chorister, since the Church placed within his reach the chance of being elected and of occupying a position of power and authority in the cathedral for a day at least, and of being the recipient, if he were so fortunate, of a very large sum of money, with perhaps the chance of a lengthy trip around the diocese for entertainment and even greater perks. To varying degrees the same privileges would be accorded to those in schools, colleges and monasteries. For a young boy, the chance to be made "bishop" must have held some of the same excitement as a modern lottery win. Even for those boys who never achieved the status of Boy Bishop there was the opportunity to participate in the festivities.

The election for the Boy Bishop generally took place on the day or on the eve of St Nicholas, 6th December, although the practice did vary. At Eton despite a provision in the statutes of the school that the election should take place on 6th December, the scholars' election had begun to be held on St Hugh's Day.[2] Here, Malim, an Elizabethan headmaster, described the office as the "Bishop of Nothingness" (*Episcopus Nihilensis*), possibly a caustic comment on the affair, but in all likelihood an unintentional error in transcribing *Episcopus Nicolatensis* (Nicholas Bishop) – an alternative name.[3]

The choristers at Salisbury were careful to maintain their right to elect the Boy Bishop themselves and followed a regulated procedure in which scrutators were appointed to oversee the election, collecting both oral and written votes. There was a more festive election held in Magdalen College, Oxford where *"on the even of St. Nicholas, an entertainment at the expense of the college was served up to the choristers in the hall, at which the chaplains as clerks were also present, and occasionally the fellows. The Boy Bishop was then chosen and presented with gloves, &c. as marks of dignity"*.[4] The election was suspended in 1405 at Finchale Abbey as the result of the wars.[5] There is also notice of elections at Toul, where he was elected by the choristers and subdeacons after Compline on the First Sunday in Advent,[6] at Laon and in Franconia where both he and his deacons were elected.[7]

Yet it is clear that the selection of the Boy Bishop by choristers' vote was not universally popular, especially among the cathedral clergy, who, as we shall see, had something to lose if the "wrong" boy was elected. And it is not unlikely that, whether out of a spirit of mischief, malice or ignorance, the choristers might well elect a boy who was prepared to captain and inspire their misbehaviour to the annoyance and discomfort of those in authority. The chance of settling scores, even if temporarily, with those under whose discipline they had suffered for the year must have proved too powerful a temptation to resist for many boys.

Accordingly, attempts were made to remove the choristers' free choice. In 1449 at Salisbury, the precentor, Nicholas Upton, following the disturbances and murder of the previous year, tried to impose a new system on the choristers: he gave them the choice of three boys: Thacham, Knyton and Bokebynder, no doubt all worthy, sensible and well-behaved boys, the type of boys who make a schoolmaster's life easy. It is not possible to say whether the choristers objected to these boys personally, or because they thought their position to be compromised, or simply because there was a deep-rooted objection to the clergy interfering in their affairs, but, in any event, the choristers refused to accept such an imposition, and a meeting of the cathedral canons was called by the dean. After much argument, the votes cast showed that the precentor was alone in trying to enforce the change. Ironically, Upton's politically naïve challenge had the opposite effect to the one he had intended. The boys' position was strengthened with the decree that no one might interfere with the choristers' choice and election. They could choose any of their number to be their *episcopus puerorum*.[8] It must have been an uncomfortable time for Thacham, Knyton and Bokebynder.

Had he only been aware of it, Upton might have looked north for a more subtle line of attack. In 1367 the clergy of York Minster successfully adopted a more crafty approach, thus avoiding the mistake made by Upton of directly imposing candidates, and so achieved the desired result. A statute was passed laying down the requirements that the boy elected should be the one who had served longest in the church and who was the most suitable, with the proviso that he be suitably good-looking. Failure to elect such a boy would invalidate the election.[9] These qualifications seem objective and fair enough, yet the astute clergy had taken control of the election, for who but they would be arbiters of the "most suitable" boy? The lack of any recorded opposition suggests that the choristers accepted the inevitable and elected boys who would be acceptable to the canons, or at least acquiesced when their elections were deemed invalid. The requirement that the boy be good-looking indicates that visual drama was deemed to be important. Strangely, it seems that at some time a chorister who could not sing, or at least could not sing properly, had been elected, for a further condition was added in 1399 that he should have a good voice. Given the prominence of the Boy Bishop in the cathedral services a boy with a poor voice would have been something of an embarrassment. In places such as parish churches where the office of the Boy Bishop was not regulated by statute there is ample reason for assuming that the clergy kept a tighter grip on proceedings.

However, the election could create other types of trouble. For instance, at Noyon in 1430, two Boy Bishops were elected, one the legitimate cathedral Bishop, the other being elected in St Martin's church. The schoolmaster was called to account over the affair by the cathedral chapter and was asked to accept that the Boy Bishop's election was their prerogative,[10] such was the prestige of such an election.

In all likelihood election problems were averted at Rheims cathedral where the choristers elected a Boy Archbishop who went solemnly to the chapter to be confirmed as being suitable to hold the office and to receive the customary rewards. He was allowed to choose his officers, including a butler who was usually the richest and most willing.[11]

The excitement of the election over, the boys could now look forward to a colourful and exciting variation from the typical daily round. For some this would come on 6th December, St Nicholas's day itself, which remained the focus of celebration, while most others would look forward to the feast of Holy Innocents on 28th December as the day when the Boy Bishop would assume his office. For a cathedral chorister the festivities might not be restricted to just a single day, but might well spread over a period of several days or longer, presenting a much needed festive glow to the winter season.

The study of medieval kingship, the feudal system, and the overall structure of society gives a general picture of an authoritarian method of governing. Yet the election of the Boy Bishop is a reminder of the more democratic strands that undoubtedly existed, certainly within the monasteries but also within the broader Church, if not so strongly within society at large. This is not to claim that it was democracy as we understand it. In the cathedrals, for example, the choristers by-and-large came from wealthy, if not noble, families, for few others could afford to pay for such an education and to lose a valuable pair of hands as well. Despite the limitations, the Church did offer a type of meritocracy and the chance for a boy or young man to achieve success with the support of his fellows. The rejection of the clergy choices for Boy Bishop at Salisbury is illustrative of a determination to be found elsewhere in medieval society to defend those privileges which acted as a means to soften or negate authority imposed from above.

The Boy Bishop Ceremonies

Framed in the arches of the cathedral, amid the polychrome glories of the statues and decorations, the elected boy prepared for the great celebration, the liturgical drama, which generally took place on the eve of Holy Innocents' Day, although the liturgical celebrations would continue during Holy Innocents' Day itself. It should be remembered that as far as Church celebrations were concerned a feast day would commence on the evening of the preceding day. In much the same way as Midnight Mass holds a particular place in the affections of contemporary congregations, the elaborate celebrations of the Boy Bishop, as darkness began to fall, with the impressive ceremonial, the candle-lit church, the beautiful chants, the processions by candlelight, the gorgeous robes and the sight and sound of the young boy leading proceedings, would have made a bright and indelible impression on the mind. It was fortuitous that the organisation of the liturgical day allowed for the main ceremony of the *episcopus puerorum* to be conducted at dusk, when the illuminated glory of the church or cathedral would offer a comforting and uplifting contrast to the bleakness of the winter night. Even today, when the ubiquitous electric light has banished darkness from the streets and corners of our cities, it is still possible to be impressed by the glow of a warmly lit building standing firm against a frosty night sky. How much more impressive would a cathedral, designed to echo heaven itself in its beauty, have been to one in the Middle Ages stepping into its light.

In an age when literacy was far from universal, the Church was accustomed to use its liturgies to impress and inform. The ceremonies of the Boy Bishop had this rationale. The audience was a wide one: choristers and clerics of all ranks, and in the congregation rich and poor, children and adults. Dean Geoffrey de Feringues[1] of St. Paul's understood that the ceremonies not only laid emphasis on the children martyred by King Herod following the birth of Christ, but revealed the importance of children by presenting them as central characters in the drama of the liturgy. In addition, the boy should be seen to represent the innocent Christ leading his flock.

…on the feast of Holy Innocents, on which they shed their blood for the innocent Christ, an innocent Boy Bishop should perform the office, so that in this way a boy would be in charge of boys and an innocent command the innocent, preserving his image in the Church, whom the innocent follow wherever he goes.[2]

At Salisbury, too, this was made explicit: *"the Boy Bishop representing the boy Christ, the true and eternal"*.[3] In fact, the visually striking reality of a young boy taking the place of a bishop and leading an important service, accompanied by the complete ceremonial of candles, vestments, incense, chants and processions would have reinforced Christ's teachings that *"… the last shall be first, and the first last"*,[4] and *"Truly I say to you, unless you change and become as little children, you shall not enter the kingdom of heaven. Therefore, whoever humbles himself like this child is the greatest in the kingdom of heaven. And whoever welcomes a little child like this in my name welcomes me"*.[5] An innocent leading the innocent is a notion found again in Erasmus's sermon for a Boy Bishop. Thus, the boy was expected to set a Christ-like pattern for the other boys, while his displacing of the real bishop illustrated the truth that even the powerful rule only on the sufferance of the Almighty who *"hath put down the mighty from their seat and hath exalted the humble and meek"*.[6] In an unmistakable fashion, the ceremonies showed that children were not to be ignored, that they had an important position and role, whilst in addition they possessed virtues too often forgotten by adults. The clerics would also have been well-aware that many boy choristers were destined to be the future priests and bishops of the Church and that the boyish impulse to dress up and play-act might be coaxed into a belief that the staff of a true and faithful bishop would not always be beyond the grasp of the small hand that clutched the facsimile.

> *And lerne as fast as thou can*
> *For our bishop is an old man*
> *And therfor thou must learn fast*
> *If thou wilt be bishop when he is past.*[7]

A story told about the early life of St Athanasius would have reinforced the belief that a boy who imitated a bishop might aspire to become one. The Bishop of Alexandria, Alexander, is said to have been looking out of his window one day watching a group of children at play on the beach, when he noticed one of the boys taking the part of a bishop performing the rite of Baptism. He summoned the children and on questioning them concluded that a valid baptism had in fact taken place, and so he completed the ceremony by an anointing with holy oil. He was so impressed with the understanding and earnestness of the little boy playing bishop that he took him into his own court. Athanasius later became secretary to the bishop and finally in 326 Bishop of Alexandria himself, gaining lasting fame for his opposition to the Arian heresy.

Salisbury (the general detail of the ceremonies)

The ceremony at Salisbury on the eve of Holy Innocents was indeed a splendid affair.[8]

A Note on Ceremonial at Salisbury

Until the Council of Trent authorised a missal for universal use in 1570, based on the Roman Rite, there were several liturgical rites in use. The Salisbury Rite (Sarum Use) was the most important and influential in England, which is strange considering that Salisbury was not one of the most prominent dioceses. However, the importance of Sarum was probably established following the Norman Conquest with the desire of the new rulers to impose a more Norman tradition on the pattern of Rouen. For those who have had some experience of the Old Latin Mass, it may also come as somewhat of a surprise to learn that the Sarum Use was generally more elaborate and flamboyant than its Roman neighbour and that, had it not been abolished during the Reformation, it would have remained (like some other rites) a permitted option to the authorised missal.

Before Vespers began the choristers were dressed in magnificent silk copes and the Boy Bishop himself was arrayed in the even more elaborate and beautiful robes of the bishop.

During Vespers the choristers carrying lighted candles went in procession with the Boy Bishop either to the altar of the Holy Innocents or to the altar of the Holy Trinity and All Saints, singing as they went. The Boy Bishop would begin the chant with words taken from the Apocalypse.[9]

> *The hundred and forty-four thousand which were redeemed from the earth. These are they which were not defiled with women, for they remained virgins. Thus may they reign with God and the Lamb and the Lamb of God with them.*

To which three other choristers responded:

> *These were redeemed from among all men, the first fruits to God and*
> *to the Lamb, and in their mouth was found no guile. Thus may they*
> *reign with God and the Lamb and the Lamb of God with them.*

It might seem an odd text at first sight, if only because it suggests that Herod slew 144,000 infants. But that is to take it too literally; it simply proposed that the children were redeemed because of their innocence. They were regarded as martyrs above all others by virtue of being slaughtered not merely for the Faith but for the person of the infant Christ himself. The pure voices of the three young boys echoing around the cathedral singing about the death of the infant children were obviously intended to create an emotional effect.

Then followed the singing of *Sedentem* with the clear indication that this was more than just a simple chant and that elementary harmony was employed, for the boys were instructed to hold the note of the final "e" of each Latin line while the response *"Thus they reign"* was sung.

Sitting in the height of heaven's majesty	*Sedentem in superne maiestatis arce__e*
Humbly they worship, crying out to you	*Adorant humilime proclamantes ad te__e*
Holy, Holy, Holy, King of Sabaoth	*Sancte, Sancte, Sancte, Sabaoth rex__e*
All things are full of your glory	*Plena sunt omnia gloriae tue__e*
With them the twenty-four	*Cum illis undeviginti quinque__e*
And with the most innocent flock	*Atque cum innocentissimo grege__e*
Who are without any stain	*Qui sunt sine ulla labe__e*
Saying in a loud voice	*Dicentes excelsa voce__e*
Praise be, to you, O Lord,	*Laus Tibi, Domine__e*
King of Eternal Glory.	*Rex eterne glorie__e.*
(Response to each line) Thus they reign.	*(Chorus respondeat) Ideo regnant.*

While this was being sung, the Boy Bishop incensed the altar and the image of the Holy Trinity so that the smoke might rise to heaven like prayers. It is likely that he was assisted in this by two boys holding the edges of his cope allowing him to swing the thurible freely. The significance of this ceremonial would obviously have been greater if the choice of altar had fallen on that of the Holy Innocents but it is not possible to tell what guided the decision.

The censing completed, the boy said in a subdued voice:

Rejoice in the Lord and be glad you righteous.

To which the choir replied:

And give glory all you that are good in heart.

Next there followed a prayer said by the Boy Bishop, stressing the importance of purity, without the introduction *Dominus vobiscum*, for, at least at Salisbury, the canons were careful to give the boy no spiritual function that was solely the preserve of the priesthood.

> *O God, whose innocent martyrs on this very day confessed their praise not in their words but in their deaths, mortify in us all the ills of sin that your faith, which we utter with our tongues, may be proclaimed by our lives in our deeds. Who lives and reigns with God the Father and the same Holy Spirit, world without end. Amen.*

The procession back to the high altar was accompanied by another chant, a responsory of the Blessed Virgin Mary, intoned by the boy acting as precentor[10] and taken up by the rest of the choir.

> *Happy are you, holy maiden Mary, and most worthy of all praise, since out of you is risen the Sun of Righteousness, Christ our God.*
>
> *Pray for your people, intervene for your clergy, intercede for women that are faithful; let them all know comfort who celebrate your feast day.*
>
> *Since out of you is risen the Sun of Righteousness, Christ our God.*
>
> *Glory be to the Father and to the Son and to the Holy Spirit; as it*

was in the beginning, is now and ever shall be, world without end. Amen.

Since out of you is risen the Sun of Righteousness, Christ our God.

The boys having arrived at the high altar through the west gate, another highly symbolic piece of liturgical theatre was presented as they took their places in the higher stalls, the place of honour; and from this time until the procession of the following day none of the clergy was allowed in these stalls. In the most literal way, the boys could now look down on their superiors. There were strict rules for the procession mentioned above and the boys taking the places of the priests were allowed to distribute the more lowly jobs among the cathedral clergy: the greater dignitaries to assist in carrying the thurible and bearing the book, the lesser in carrying the candles.

The singing of the responsory having being completed, the Boy Bishop took the bishop's seat and said in a subdued voice:

Beautiful in form before the sons of men.

To which the choristers responded:

Grace is spread on your lips.

There is probably a deliberate ambiguity here. On the one hand, it might be supposed that the Christ Child is being described as beautiful in form, but on the other, the words might easily be applied to the boy himself, beautiful in his innocence. Perhaps the regulation at York stipulating that the boy be *"good-looking"* echoes this.

Next, the boy addressed a further prayer to the Blessed Virgin and prayed for peace and received the response.

O God, who by the fruitful virginity of Mary ever blessed has furnished humankind with the reward of salvation, grant we beseech you that we know she intercedes for us, through whom we are worthy to receive the Author of Life. Who lives and reigns with you in the unity of the Holy Spirit, world without end. Amen.

Peace be with you.

And with your spirit.

Two or three canons then said:

Let us bless the Lord.

The cross-bearer next took the Boy Bishop's staff and began the antiphon, facing the Boy Bishop:

Prince of the Church, Shepherd of the Sheep, deign to give your blessing to all your people. (Turning to the people.) In meekness and love humble yourselves to receive the blessing.

To which the choir responded:

Thanks be to God.

The cross-bearer returned the staff to the Boy Bishop and there then followed the several parts of the blessing with the choir responding:

Our help is in the name of the Lord. (The Boy Bishop making the sign of the cross on his forehead.)

Who has made heaven and earth.

Blessed be the name of the Lord. (Making the sign of the cross on his chest.)

From this time forth for evermore.

I sign you with the sign of the cross (With arm raised). Let it be our defence. (Turning to the people.) Who has purchased and redeemed us (turning back to the altar) with the price of his flesh. (Turning back and placing his hand on his breast.)

Amen.

It seems that Compline, the last service of the day, began without a break. This followed the usual pattern and concluded with another blessing.

> *Our help is in the name of the Lord. (The Boy Bishop making the sign of the cross on his forehead.)*
>
> *Who made heaven and earth.*
>
> *Blessed be the name of the Lord. (Making the sign of the cross on his chest.)*
>
> *From this time forth for evermore.*
>
> *May Almighty God, the Father, the Son and the Holy Spirit bless us.*
>
> *Amen.*

Again it is worth noting that since strictly only priests could say *bless you*, the boy used the layman's blessing *bless us*. In this way Salisbury carefully maintained a determinedly orthodox theology, and with this blessing the liturgies for the day concluded.

The following day was the feast of Holy Innocents itself and if this day fell on a Sunday further ceremonial was prescribed for the offices of the day, repeating some of the chants, psalms and responsories already seen, with an emphasis on purity, innocence and martyrdom.

The procession followed much the same pattern as before, beginning with *The hundred and forty-four thousand, These were redeemed* and *Thus may they reign*, except that three boys only sang the prose *Sedentem* and they finished at a station before the cross.

At Matins at the third nocturn, after the lessons, all the boys begin the Nones responsory on the altar step which included again: *The hundred and forty-four thousand,* and *These were redeemed, Glory be to the Father,* and *Thus may they reign.*

There then followed:

> *The righteous, however, shall live for ever and their reward is with God.[11] Glory be… The saints will rejoice in glory and will be joyful in their beds.[12]*

At Lauds, after *Laudate*,[13] the Boy Bishop still vested in the silk cope, worn throughout the day, read the Little Chapter.

> *I looked and I saw the Lamb standing on Mount Zion and with him the one hundred and forty-four thousand having his name and the name of the Father written on their foreheads.*

Next came the hymn *Glorious King of Martyrs* [14] and then:

> *God is terrible from out his sanctuary. The God of Israel himself gives strength and mightiness to his people. Blessed be God! [15]*

There followed a repetition of *These are they which were not defiled with women* and the *Benedictus* [16] with a repeat of the prayer *O God, whose innocent martyrs*. The office ended with the Boy Bishop giving the same blessing as he had already given at Vespers, three short prayers[17] and another blessing in the same form as he had given at the end of Compline.

The end of the Boy Bishop's tenure came with Vespers in the evening of the feast of the Holy Innocents, which followed a similar pattern to the Vespers of the previous day, except that when *The hundred and forty thousand* was chanted it was sung by one boy alone dressed in a silk cope, who was performing the role of chancellor. The rest of the choristers were now vested merely in surplices. The ecclesiastical ceremonies concluded for the year with the form of blessing that had ended the previous day's Vespers. The Sarum Use did not include the second *Deposuit* [18] as the Boy Bishop relinquished his post, another symbolic piece of ceremonial that was to be found elsewhere. Until Archbishop Peckham's reform they were granted an *octave* [19] continuing the ceremonies for a further week, which makes clear the importance placed upon them.

Perhaps, as the ceremonies drew to a close, the boy might reflect on his day of glory or perhaps he might have begun to consider whether he and his fellows had deported themselves in such a way that would bring down retribution from their seniors and masters on the morrow; or there again, being an eternal optimist, as boys often are, he might have hoped to escape the consequences of any unseemly behaviour. At all events, it was a day in a young boy's life never to be forgotten.

Although the ceremonies of the Boy Bishop followed a roughly similar pattern across Europe, there was no completely standard liturgical form; however, many features of the Salisbury rite were common. In some cathedrals the drama was more impressive or more flamboyant, perhaps to a modern mind even lacking in taste, while in others it had a harder edge. We should not be surprised at these variations, for despite the control exercised by the Church, there was no attempt to impose a complete uniformity of practice. Local customs flourished with borrowings and adaptations, and we shall not call the Middle Ages a neat and tidy period. Conforming to a pattern did not require an exact reproduction; orthodoxy did not insist on uniformity.

Exeter (showing some variation)

The powerful influence of the Sarum Use can be identified in the Boy Bishop liturgies at Exeter.[20] Here can be seen not only the same broad elements, such as the procession of the boys (in this case to the top of the *pulpitum* – the massive stone screen dividing the choir from the nave – where the Boy Bishop censed the Great Crucifix), the vestments and the blessing, but also in the great similarities in the prayers and chants; for example: *The one hundred and forty-four thousand, These were redeemed, Sitting in the height* were used. The offices on the feast of Holy Innocents bear very marked similarities too.

York (skilful and confident boys required)

From the York Missal[21] we are given the roles of the Boy Bishop and his choristers at Mass on the feast of Holy Innocents. An unusual injunction was laid upon the boy at York directing him to assist the treasurer to collect the *cirpos* [22] for Christmas and Epiphany.[23] Appropriately enough, the Mass of the day commenced with *"Out of the mouths of babes and sucklings you have fashioned praise because of your enemies"* [24] which was followed soon after by *"of course"* a group of boys standing in the middle of the choir[25] singing the *Kyries*. Meanwhile the Boy Bishop was seated in glory on the bishop's throne. If the day were a Sunday, after the *Kyries*, the boy would intone the beginning of the *Gloria* and perhaps chant the collect.[26] Three boys standing in the middle of the choir chanted the *Gradale: "Our soul has escaped like a sparrow from the snare of the hunter. The snare is broken and we are delivered. The white-robed army of martyrs praises you, O God"*. There followed a long *Sequentia* sung by the precentor of the boys, that related in quite horrifying detail the slaughter of the Innocents and, contrasted this with their heavenly reward which the boy prayed might also be received by all present.[27] A confident and skilful boy it was to agree to perform this solo. While the stipulation was made in 1399 that the Boy Bishop had to have a good voice, it is also evident that the boy performing this role required one too, with the necessary intelligence and patience to learn the music. It would be an anxious moment, especially for the cleric who had trained him, as he intoned the first notes. This boy precentor would certainly have earned his share of festivities outside the liturgy. Before the gospel, the deacon sought a blessing from the Boy Bishop in the same way as he would from the true bishop and the Mass continued as usual.

St. Paul's, London (the higher clergy avoid some of the indignities)

Without doubt the ceremonies of the Boy Bishop were firmly established at St Paul's. An ordinance in the statues of 1263 refers to the office of the Boy Bishop which was already said to be in accordance with ancient custom.[28] As at Salisbury, the boys had been allowed that wonderful chance to choose whatever clergy they wished to perform the more menial tasks during the services. Unfortunately, in a way reminiscent of the sort of squabbles expected between the boys themselves, this had caused friction between the higher and lower clergy over carrying the thurible, candles and other duties. In order to bring some measure of order to the quarrelsome clergy it was decided that the most senior clergy would be exempt from being thus used by the boys. Although such a pronouncement would hardly be welcomed by the choristers, who would have obviously delighted in watching their seniors perform the tasks that they themselves usually performed throughout the year, keen to pick fault and criticise, it is not surprising that the senior clergy tried to extricate themselves from a potentially demeaning set of tasks, only to leave the clergy of the lower ranks to bear the burden. Perhaps the boys had previously taken things too far in this cathedral, for it was further stipulated that the boys must dress and sing in a seemly fashion befitting a decent procession. It is not hard to imagine the sort of irreverence the boys might have introduced given that they felt that they were celebrating their feast and that at least some of the usual rules were suspended.

By the time of Dean Colet things must have been far more dignified and controlled. When he founded St Paul's school he laid down in the statute of 1518 that *"All these children shall, every Childermas Daye (an old name for Holy Innocents), come to Paule's church, and hear the Childe Bishop's sermone; and after be at the hyghe mass, and each of them offer 1d. to the Childe Bishop, and with them maistors and surveyors of the scole"*.[29] These rather surprising sermons will be examined later; but bearing in mind the content of Erasmus's sermon for the Boy Bishop, it appears that even the reforming Colet, who had little time for the perceived excesses of the medieval church, maintained the age-old belief that it would be instructive for the boys to see the example of a boy leading boys and to be lectured on Christian behaviour. Thus, he seized the educational opportunity offered and marched the boys to the ceremonies.

Hereford

There is far less detail than can be found for some of the other cathedrals, although it seems that the boys at least had the usual procession.[30]

France – Rouen (how the Deposuit worked)

It is unsurprising that the ceremonial order of Rouen bears a close similarity to that of Salisbury, since it is likely that Rouen had had a powerful influence on the Sarum Use.[31] After Vespers on the evening before Holy Innocents, the choristers with the Boy Bishop processed from the vestry two-by-two, a pair dressed in tunicles and the rest in copes, all carrying candles. They sang *The one hundred and forty-four thousand*. And then at the altar of the Holy Innocents three boys sang *These were redeemed*. Indeed, the whole structure including the final blessing followed the same lines as at Salisbury. These boys were accorded an unusual privilege, however, for they themselves were allowed to decide the importance of the feast of Holy Innocents: they could leave it as a *double* or make it a more important *triple*. Again, the actual celebrations for the feast of Holy Innocents, the offices and the Mass, were remarkably similar to what we have already seen at Salisbury and York. However, the Rouen ceremonies made provision for the *Deposuit* during the last Vespers of the Boy Bishop's tenure. At Vespers the *Magnificat* [32] is sung and at Rouen during the singing of the words *"Deposuit potentes de sede"* (He has put down the mighty from their seat) the Boy Bishop would hand over his staff to someone else. While the previous day he had given a lesson in humility to the cathedral clergy (and the bishop too, if he were there) by taking the bishop's seat and dressing himself in the robes of the bishop, now he too was seen formally relinquishing power and position to become a boy chorister once more.

France – Bayeux (a different way of handing on to the next Boy Bishop)

Although the subject of the vestments and episcopal insignia will be considered in a later chapter, the inventory of the cathedral treasures compiled at Bayeux in 1476 [33] will give us an inkling of how grand the Boy Bishop ceremonies were and the importance that they held in the medieval Church. For the use of the Boy Bishop himself were included two mitres (at least one of which was richly embroidered with four images), a pastoral staff and gloves, while the choristers were provided with four red (or possibly cloth of gold) copes. Since the Boy Bishop could not wear two mitres at once, this list seems to indicate that there was a best and second best that could be used according to the solemnity of the liturgy, or that a second had been bought to replace an earlier one no longer regarded as suitably grand. Although at Bayeux the Boy Bishop was not allowed to wear an episcopal ring, he wore a silk tunicle as well as a cope, and was given his own boy chaplain. The Boy Bishop was instructed to perform the duties of a priest for all the offices of the feast, except Mass, in the way that we have already seen.[34] It was also laid down that the Boy Bishop should be attended by his chaplain with two candles burning in front of him. The provisions regarding the candles make interesting reading as they reveal the importance and value of candles which were regarded as a luxury item.

> *Just as at other festivals, the sacristan keeps the remains of the candles*
> *for the use of those who look after them and receives twelve pence*
> *from the hand of the Boy Bishop.*

As elsewhere, the impressive procession began after Vespers when the boys vested in silk copes went in procession with their precentor, identifiable by his amice, skullcap and staff, singing *The one hundred and forty-four thousand* not in this case to the altar of the Holy Innocents, but to the equally appropriate altar of St Nicholas. *Sitting in the height* was also sung, as was *The saints sang a new song*.[35] The *Magnificat* with its antiphon *The innocent babes* [36] and the prayer *O God, whose innocent martyrs* followed. At Bayeux, even the boys who were not choristers were not excluded from the fun, for when the Boy Bishop took the dean's stall, they were allowed to join the choristers in claiming the seats of the clergy.

There is a delightful description of what happened at the conclusion of Compline. The Boy Bishop, still vested with his pastoral staff and gloves with his mitre on his head, was serenaded back to his lodgings by the choristers, having taken off their silk copes, singing *Sedentem*. Many parents, familiar with the reluctance of children to take off their favourite clothes, be they playsuits or football kit, will understand the concession made to the youth of the Boy Bishop, for he was given permission to wear his mitre and surplice until they all went to sleep. Similarly, it was appointed that the next day the boys were to go to the cathedral singing the appointed text and return with the Boy Bishop vested with gloves, mitre and staff.

The ceremonies for this day are broadly similar to what we have already seen,[37] except it seems that Boy Bishop for the following year would already have been chosen before Vespers on the feast of Holy Innocents. During the singing of the *Magnificat*, at the *Deposuit*, a strange variation of usual practice was to be seen. The choristers moved to the middle of the church, standing in order as though in procession, and the Boy Bishop offered his pastoral staff to his chorister companions until it reached the boy elected for the following year. After many repetitions of the *Deposuit* line, they returned to the choir leading the Boy Bishop to the altar, singing the *Te Deum*. Here the new Bishop was vested in his silk cope and mitre and given his staff.[38] The Boy Bishop whom he was to replace would be his chaplain next year. A new cantor would be elected. There is no indication of how the Boy Bishop was elected, but it seems certain that the process must have been settled long before Vespers began, since if the appointment hinged upon the decision of the Boy Bishop himself during Vespers it is not hard to imagine, if not a scene of fighting and sulking, at least an unholy set of boyish solicitations, bargaining, pleading, arguing, begging and threatening, taking place in the cathedral. And since the ordinances stated that the Boy Bishop offered his staff to his companions, it is probably not too much to suggest that this ceremony was carefully orchestrated, each boy being given the staff in turn and then returning it, until it was placed in the hand of the selected boy. After the investiture of the new Boy Bishop, the *Magnificat* was sung from the beginning. At the end of Vespers the new Boy Bishop gave the blessing in the usual way.

France – Coutances (extra licence for the boys)

At Coutances the ceremony was conducted with even more dignity.[39] After Matins came the delight, eagerly awaited by the boys, of drawing up the job-sheet for the liturgies, with the exciting freedom to assign tasks to both higher and lower clergy. The deacons and subdeacons could expect to look after the incense and the larger or smaller candles, but even better, the boys could put the cantor, the canons or even the true bishop in charge of the fire, water, missal, gloves or bell. Although it was stated that nothing dishonourable or impertinent was to be organised, the older men being placed first on the list, the younger last, there was plenty of scope for mischievous boys who felt harshly treated to place unpopular clergy in demeaning positions.

After the Vespers of the eve of Holy Innocents, all the choristers and those not ordained gathered behind the high altar to vest the Boy Bishop in amice, stole, tunic, silk cope, mitre, gloves, ring and staff and to set themselves in order for the procession. Vespers concluded, the Boy Bishop began *O quam gloriosum* [40] which was then sung as the procession went out, the thurifers[41] and candlebearers first, then those not in sacred orders, followed by the choir in silk copes holding candles. After these came the rest, two-by-two, also holding candles, the true cantor[42] in a silk cope, with the most recent Bishop preceded by the larger candle-bearers, two clergy of the second stall who were called chaplains, in silk copes, and with his chaplain on the right and the deputy chaplain on the left, also in silk copes. Thus in order they left through the great door to the choir and went via the right side of the cathedral and crossed to the left. Then changing direction they processed up the right side of the cathedral to the middle of the nave where they made a station. Here the Boy Bishop was censed by his two chaplains, who then kissed his hand. After this, thurifers censed the choir to left and right. The antiphons, psalm, prayers and blessing finished, the procession returned to the choir where the Boy Bishop ascended to the bishop's seat accompanied by his two chaplains while the choristers claimed their places in the higher stalls reserved for the clergy.

The canon who was responsible for carrying the book of collects during Compline was precisely identified as one who held a particular clerical post. Indeed the carrying of this book for the Boy Bishop was regarded as an honour attaching to the prebend. The canon was also given the right to take the candle that had burned before the Boy Bishop for his own use, a valuable benefit, given the high price of candles. After the conclusion of Compline the boy, having removed his vestments, was escorted back to his lodgings by the choir led by two candle-bearers, accompanied by their singing *Greatly rejoicing*. In the same manner he was also led back after Matins and the Mass of the following day.

The Coutances' ceremonial is stipulated in precise detail both for the eve and the feast of the Holy Innocents. There are not only careful descriptions about when the Boy Bishop should be vested in episcopal robes but also how this should take place. The different parts sung by the different sections of the choir are clearly stated as are all the ceremonial movements.[43] At Mass the Boy Bishop joined the priest for the prayers at the foot of the altar at the beginning of Mass, he blessed the deacon or priest who read the Gospel and kissed the text, and blessed the incense. At the Offertory the priest turned to the Boy Bishop so that he might bless the chalice.

The boy's tenure concluded with the *Deposuit* during the Vespers on the day of Holy Innocents, as in many other places, but here his pastoral staff was laid on the altar and the boy was accompanied or perhaps carried to his residence by the rest of the boys.

France – Toul (a darker part of the ceremony)

In the main, the ceremonies at Toul[44] matched those at Coutances, except that here the outgoing bishop was given the privilege of electing a canon to organise the event the following year.[45] One of the duties laid upon this canon was that he must provide a supper for the Boy Bishop on the evening of the feast of Holy Innocents. This canon was also expected to thank the Boy Bishop and to ask to be excused if he had in any way failed anyone. He then handed the Boy Bishop a cap of rosemary or a mixture of other flowers which would be presented to another canon who would thus be responsible for the ceremonies in the succeeding year. However, if the canon (or his deputy) was perceived to have failed in his duties, he would be subjected to a cruel piece of ritual humiliation, for the boys were allowed to place a black cope on a stick in the middle of the choir, where it would remain to spite him, as long as the ferial subdeacons and the boys pleased. Furthermore they did not have to obey the cathedral authorities in this matter. What is worse, the offending canon was prevented from receiving any of the emoluments of his office until he had made amends for his insult to the choir. No doubt most canons dreaded this selection by rosemary cap which would give the Boy Bishop another means of exacting retribution for past severities and they would be especially careful to discharge their duties to the boys with the utmost care and consideration.

Cambrai – France (the Boy Bishop is given a surprising authority)

John Gregory, quoting Molanus, relates that in the church of Cambrai the Boy Bishop was allowed to appoint a priest to an important cathedral post (a prebend) which had fallen vacant during his period of office.[46] This would be power indeed, well beyond what most Boy Bishops could dream of exercising. It is probably, however, safe to assume that the boy did not take this decision unaided, and it is certainly not impossible that it was found convenient to use the boy to announce a decision that had been made by the proper authority, since he was nominally in charge. According to Rigollot the same privilege attended the Boy Bishop at Beauvais.[47] As we shall see later, it was commonly believed that much the same power was vested in the Boy Bishop of Mainz, although this belief was mistaken.

Germany (a marvellous and irreverent celebration for the boys)

There are detailed accounts about how the ceremonies were performed from the school side.[48] In Germany, the boys might well have looked forward to the feast of Holy Innocents with even greater anticipation than their counterparts in the rest of Europe, for in most monastery schools the masters on that day refrained from beating their pupils in view of the honour given to children by the feast. It could well be that those masters, more sensitively aware of the brutality of Herod's Massacre of the Innocents, felt that it was somehow improper to beat their own charges on that day. Perhaps they wanted not even the slightest association with Herod to taint their consciences. This was part of the widely observed tradition that the masters and pupils changed roles for the day; the bishop and his chapter, the abbot and his monks left the running of the school to the pupils, who also officiated, as we have seen, in church. It would have been an unwise boy, however, who took too great an advantage of the licence of that day, for there was always the day after when the masters' consciences would be softened and their arms strengthened, ready to deal with the insolent and unruly.

The Abbey of St Gall, where the visit of King Conrad has already been noted, had a unique method of conducting the ceremonial. As early as the Sunday before St Catherine's Day (25th November) the boys elected their Abbot, who would then choose two of his fellows to assist him as chaplains.[49] After ascending the throne by climbing on a table, they received the homage of the other boys, who sang the hymn *Behold, behold, a virgin gives birth to God* and gave gifts of bread and wine. Although he did not officially begin his office until the feast of Holy Innocents, the Boy Abbot was led into church with great ceremony and the singing of hymns on the eve of St Lucy's Day (13th December). At the door of the church all the boys, having removed their shoes and gowns, waited in eager anticipation for a signal. As soon as it was given the boys raced to the altar hoping to catch the Boy Abbot. If they succeeded he was not allowed to ascend the altar steps and had to forfeit four measures of wine. On the other hand, if he outran his pursuers he was afforded the privilege of sitting in an armchair until the end of the office and throwing apples, pears and flatcakes at the other boys or drenching them with water. To our mind, it seems an extraordinarily irreverent way of conducting a church service, but perhaps the association with apples went back to the time of King Conrad. As was customary in most places, the real ceremonies began after the second Vespers of St John's Day. The Boy Abbot was allowed to use a decorated prayer-stool. However, there was an addition to the ceremonies here, perhaps as a result of the importance of music at St Gall, because at the *Deposuit* during these Vespers the choirmaster of the monastery entrusted his baton to the hands of one of the boys who conducted the choir until the *Magnificat* ended. After Vespers, the boys, with Boy Abbot heading the procession, left the church and returned to his lodgings where once again he climbed onto the table with his chaplains, sang several antiphons to which the choir responded, entertained them all with dances and capers, and gave the episcopal blessing to conclude proceedings.

Again, the remaining offices of the monastic round, Mass excluded, were conducted by the boys until the office of Second Vespers on Holy Innocents' Day. The Boy Bishop, or Abbot, would sing the ninth lesson at Matins – just like the true abbot – and give blessings during his procession. Back in the school, the boys were placed in charge of the refectory and took the role of monks in reading during meals. In the school itself they *"were not bound by any law"* and, because they took full advantage of this, woe to anyone who dared enter the school, for the unlucky venturer would find himself imprisoned until he ransomed himself with a suitably large payment. For these customs to continue required a degree of good nature on the part of the adults, especially the clergy and schoolmasters, who were perhaps not always so unyielding and vicious as is sometimes suggested.

The tolerance of those in authority is well illustrated by Bishop Solomon who thought to glance into the school to see how the boys were behaving on this day. Perhaps he was all-too-aware of the mischief that boys can create. However, on seeing him, the boys shouted in unison, *"Let's capture the bishop and not the abbot!"* Having been quickly surrounded by the excited boys, the kindly bishop submitted to their authority and they pulled him onto the schoolmaster's desk. However, when seated at the desk, Solomon continued the jest and, being in the place of the schoolmaster, demanded the schoolmaster's privilege of beating them, shouting, *"Off with the habits!"* The boys immediately obeyed, but begged him to allow them to buy off the beatings, which was sometimes allowed by their real schoolmaster. The bishop enquired as to how they were able to buy off their beatings and, as an answer, the very young boys addressed him as well as they could in Latin; the intermediates spoke rhythmically; but the rest spoke metrically, even rhetorically as if in truth giving a speech. Two boys even recited the exact words spoken in the times of Ekkhart IV that were used to threaten the abbot into making an appeal to the king if he was contemplating curtailing their *"old prerogative"*. Since he was so delighted with their achievements he picked them up in turn, just as they stood in their linen shirts, embraced them with kisses and said, *"Get dressed again!"* and then added, *"Indeed, if I am granted life I want to buy myself out and reward such talent with gifts."* The gentle old man faithfully fulfilled his promise and so it is likely that the boys would look back with fondness on a bishop who had entered into the spirit of their festivity with such wit and good grace.

At Mainz, no doubt mindful of the potential for boyish misbehaviour, the authorities had decided that the boy should be selected by the schoolmaster.[50] Here he had assigned to him an entourage of several knights, a standard bearer and two chaplains with as many bedels. As Boy Bishop he made his first appearances in the cathedral at the First and Second vespers of St Nicholas and at High Mass. Although he performed no religious function before the eve of Holy Innocents, he did carry out visits to the Elector.

Italy – Padua (the inclusion of an unusual ceremony)

At Padua the ceremonial exchange of places between clergy and choir received further emphasis when the two priests removed their copes in order that a pair of boys might take them up.[51] Here the procession was directed to go to the altar of St Daniel singing *The hundred and forty-four thousand* where the altar and Boy Bishop were censed. At Mass the boy presided in his cope and mitre, accompanied by his chaplains, while the priest celebrated the Mass itself. After the epistle, the reader, dressed in a straight robe, threw a wooden spoon, which he had been holding, at the congregation. Armed men then entered who followed this spoon around the cathedral seeking the infant Christ with his mother. Three more people and a donkey now joined the drama. A cleric representing the Blessed Virgin sat on the donkey with the infant Christ on her lap.[52] St Joseph, represented by another actor, led the donkey as the Holy Family fled through the cathedral.[53] This theatrical piece of liturgy re-enacted the flight into Egypt following the warning that St Joseph had received from an angel. The flight of the Holy Family having been shown in this way, the people would have had a lively demonstration of how the infant Christ avoided the massacre of the Innocents in Bethlehem. Yet this sort of drama was by no means unusual in the medieval Church. It was used in a variety of ways and on different feasts to teach the Gospels to a largely illiterate populace. If the throwing of the wooden spoon seems a little too much like a pantomime, it ought to be remembered that this age did not view drama with our eyes. In England, for instance, people who had seen the portrayal of a drunken Noah and, in the Christmas narrative, Mack the sheep-stealer, would have seen nothing unusual in their religious education being spiced with spectacle and humour, and neither would the people of other European countries. At the offertory the boy received the people's offerings for his own use. The Sung Mass that followed was attended by the boys. During this Mass the women made offerings of money and candles for the dead boys.

Spain (very theatrical effects)

There is some evidence that in Spain the ceremonies assumed an even more spectacular form.[54] In Toledo, the Boy Bishop was elected as was usual on St Nicholas day, but his investiture was far from usual. A large cloud suspended from the vaults of the cathedral roof was lowered, on which was clustered a large company of angels (who can be assumed to be choristers). When the cloud was standing over the Boy Bishop's head, the angels leaning out from it vested the Boy Bishop in his mitre and gave him other episcopal insignia while he knelt on a specially constructed stage.[55] In other places, such as Huesca, both the Boy Bishop and another boy to represent King Herod were elected together. But the Spanish were accustomed to this type of drama, a good example of which is afforded by an Easter play performed in Mallorca. This included, in addition to a priest dressed in white alb, green velvet dalmatic and red mantle taking the part of the Mary Magdalene, an angel with his wings lit up by candles high up in the church accompanied by the discharge of a bombard.[56] This play also boasted a scene from the Last Judgement representing the dead rising from their graves, portrayed by seven or eight choristers who rolled out from beneath the altar dressed in white surplices to indicate their grave shrouds. Mallorca, however, decided to outdo its rivals by other means and, instead of electing a Boy Bishop, they elected a Boy Pope, who was even crowned with the triple tiara.[57] It was hard to better that.

In Seville the most ancient, universal and enduring of the Christmas feasts was recognised as being that of the Boy Bishop.[58] Here it was celebrated for a long time by the students of San Miguel, the choristers and other youngsters. A clear indication is given of the ceremonies by a statute of 1512 which determined to end certain profanations and abuses that had crept in. Although the archbishop, and dean and chapter of the cathedral did not want to abolish the ceremonies, they did wish to reform them so as to end the *"stream of mockery and ridicule"*. They were keen that the ceremonies on Holy Innocents should be performed in memory of the infancy and humility of the birth of Christ with corresponding humility and devotion. The young were to give examples to the old by changing places with the clergy at the *Deposuit* sung during the *Magnificat* at Vespers on St John's Day, so that, as in other cathedrals, the Boy Bishop took the bishop's throne and the other boys occupied the higher stalls. At this point, in what appears to be the only explicit medieval example, the Boy Bishop's robes and insignia were brought to him in the order given by the dean. After the boy was robed, he incensed the altar, said a prayer and gave the blessing. While Compline was sung, the Boy Bishop went to the vestry to disrobe. After Terce the choristers with four cantors in copes formed a procession with the dean, the archdeacon of Seville and other clergy. The Boy Bishop was accompanied by his attendants, and behind him others carried the mitre and staff, with a boy lifting the skirt of his cope. At the first station of the procession four singers chanted the first verse, four choristers the second, four priests the third. Since this procession was seen very much as being performed in remembrance of the martyrdom of the Holy Innocents, the dean distributed – according to the terms of a priest's will – the substantial sum of 2,000 maravedis. Mass began as soon as the procession had returned to the choir. The Boy Bishop presided at the Mass, having the Epistle and Gospel Books brought to him and the incense for blessing. At the end of Mass the Boy gave his blessing and Sext began while he, with the attendant clergy, went to disrobe in the Chapel of San Cristobal. Anyone failing to accompany him lost his share of the money offering, unless he was the celebrant saying Mass, or his sacred minister, who were permitted to disrobe in the sacristy. Moreover, a priest who failed to carry out a task assigned to him would suffer further punishment. There followed additional arrangements for the Boy Bishop to tour the city on horseback.

Not forgetting the girls

It is only to be expected that girls would want a share in the excitement enjoyed by their brothers and so in the Abbaye-aux-Bois the girls were allowed to appropriate the clothing and dignity of the nuns, while the abbess became a simple nun. The account is given by Helen Massalaksa (about ten years old), who told the story of her day.[59] She was elected by the other girls and was permitted to choose a deputy, a cross-bearer, a chaplain and other companions. Other places were assigned by popular vote. The girls censed the real abbess, who, following the usual custom, embraced the Girl Abbess, removed her own cross and gave it to the Girl and then put the abbess's ring on the Girl's finger. The following day the Girl Abbess took up her duties. While the High Mass was sung she sat on the abbey throne. A violet velvet carpet with gold fringes for decoration added grandeur. She received the incense and kissed the paten. All the nuns heard Mass and the offices in the tribunes while the girls filled the stalls. Helen blessed the water and thought it highly amusing to see nuns of only five or six years of age. Many women came to see them in the choir and in the refectory where Helen gave a great feast with ices. All the nuns and outsiders stood in the middle of the refectory to see them dine. Each of the girls put on a solemn appearance to correspond with the habit she wore. After dinner, the nuns joined in the fun, but the girls dared not go to see Madame Rochechouart, who was in charge of all the classes, because she could not tolerate such masquerades and did not want to see anyone. As for her sister, Madame Sainte-Delphine, she found the whole thing pleasingly amusing and all went to see her in turn. Several ladies spent the afternoon with her. The Girl Abbess and her company also made a visit and what amused the ladies most of all was when suddenly the door opened and Madame Rochechouart appeared. The girls all fled. That night there was a great ceremony as the cross and the ring were returned, and the girls' habits laid aside. Although a religious establishment, clearly the abbey had adopted some of the manners and customs of high-born ladies, reflecting the social origins of the girls and the nuns.

The nuns at Godstow, near Oxford, were accustomed to recite the office and prayers for the young ones on Holy Innocents, while Carrow nunnery elected a Christmas Abbess.

Many places celebrated the election of the Boy Bishop by minting tokens. There are numerous examples with a variety of designs.[60]

Although there are accounts of the ceremonies across Europe in cathedrals, monasteries, parish churches and schools, they are not always as detailed as those given above, and in most cases do little more than confirm that the ceremonies took place in a particular church. The general philosophy and execution of the ceremonies varied but little from place to place, yet this did not prevent the stamp of local custom from giving them distinctive and lively touches. They were always designed to be dramatic and colourful in an age that was used to spectacular processions, brightly dyed clothing and extravagant behaviour.

Today, indeed, for we all pride ourselves on how much value we place on children and their opinions, it would be hard to find occasions in our society where children are given as much authority and licence as they were in the medieval Boy Bishop ceremonies.

Some Boy Bishops whose names are known	
Salisbury	*York*
(Mentioned in C. Wordsworth, p 259)	1396 John Cave (see Chapter 5)
1388 William Hardegrave	(mentioned in E F Rimbualt, p xvi)
1402 John Cournour	1416 Richard Massam
1419 John Fouler	1417 Henry Fournas
1423 Thomas Rumsey	1418 Thomas Thorp
1424 Martin Webbe	1420 de Burgh
1425 Robert Wattys	1485 Thomas Malson
1426 John Husiot	1486 John Clerk
1427 Thomas Edmund	1487 Thomas Greves
1428 Richard Greene	1488 James Beswyk
1440 John Charlynge	1503 Richard Plummer
1443 William Wayte	1537 George Nevell
1444 Henry	
1446 Thomas	*Lille*
1447 Thomas Pye	1500 Guillemot Lespine (See Introduction)
1454 Robert Bremer	
1455 John Harper	*Paris*
1464 John Clerke	1367 Bartholomew Divitis (see chapter 1)
1470 Richard Brownesor	
1471 Thomas Nuttebeam	*Péronne*
1472 Whytmersshe	1638 Desjardin (see chapter 7)
1473 Stephen Lettecombe	
	Abbaye-aux-Bois
	c.1773 Helen Massalaksa (see chapter 4)
	Seville
	1641 D Esteban Dongo (see chapter 7)

5

Feasting and Visiting

It can hardly be thought that, important and magnificent as the cathedral services undoubtedly were, to the boys these would have been the most attractive elements of their time in office. The feasting, merry-making, visitations, not to forget the release from school, would surely have been things closer to their hearts. It is commonly said that the medieval period was the Age of Faith and there probably were some serious and quite pious little boys who took religious observance very seriously, but the records do not reveal much illustrating the behaviour of these would-be young saints.

While there was much fun to be had from deposing the real bishop and clergy, and lording it over them for a day, gaining an inkling of what real authority might be like, there was no escaping the reality that to exchange the miserable grind of the schoolroom for a relentless round of church offices might not in the end seem to be such a good thing. We can imagine, therefore, that the boys would probably have had their minds fixed quite firmly on the pleasures that the day promised rather than on the spiritual side of the feast. Furthermore, if the boys were allowed a visitation of the local area or diocese, school might be forgotten for several days. Attending a meal in good company was one of the ways in which people found their entertainment, especially as it was not uncommon for music or other amusements to be offered, should the host be sufficiently wealthy. In addition, because the usual restraints were somewhat slackened in this period of topsy-turvydom, there was always the hope that there would be occasions for indulging in more high-spirited behaviour than would commonly be countenanced. Dr Rock noted that:

> It was upon this festival that some wealthy man or another of the parish would make an entertainment on the occasion for his own household, and invite his neighbours' children to come and partake of it; and of course Nicholas and his clerks sat in the highest place.[1]

Many cathedrals made provision for a choristers' feast after the appointment of the

Boy Bishop on the eve of Holy Innocents. At St Paul's it was originally stipulated that if there were a new canon he had to lead the boy who was representing him to the Almonry with torches, dancing and music and there to offer drink and entertainment to everyone.[2] On the octave day he had to wait up, ready to greet the Boy Bishop and his company with a meal and to provide them with gifts on their departure. He was permitted, if he had been kept up late, to miss Matins the following day. Later, there were precise directions about how the evening's entertainment should be conducted.[3] These directions were part of the same set of statutes that we have seen before regulating which clergy might be selected to perform the different jobs during the services. It seems that the Boy Bishop could choose with which residentiary canon he was to dine on the Eve of Holy Innocents, and in this way he was given the chance either to impose upon an unpopular canon the cost and annoyance of providing a dinner, or to select one of the more amenable clergy who might supply a pleasant evening's entertainment. However, he was warned that he had to be content with this one opportunity, for he was allowed to visit no other household. He could have as his companions to the meal two candle-bearers, whom he might choose for himself, five other boys in place of clerks and two servers who would precede the bishop with staffs, although he was given instructions about exactly who could be selected. The boy who played the part of the dean was permitted to take four boys to the dean's house, where he would also dine the following day. The rest of the boys who had taken high positions had to be content with three companions and were directed to go to the houses of their masters, while those who had taken the roles of the residentiary canons were allowed no more than two companions and likewise had to go to the houses of their masters. Come evening, there would, therefore, have been much activity around the cathedral as the various groups prepared to set out for the residences where they were to be entertained. The Boy Bishop, if he so desired, could elect to join one of the other boys at the dean's house or at the house of one of the other dignitaries or canons, thus increasing the size of the whole party.

After lunch on Holy Innocents' Day the boys gathered in the porch for their instructions. They then mounted horses to go to bless the people. The dean was under an obligation to provide a horse for the Boy Bishop and the canons had to provide mounts for the boys who had represented them.

These plans might seem rather detailed and over-prescriptive but it must have been a great deal easier to control the throng of boys if they were separated into smaller groups for these feasts. It perhaps also allowed greater control over the groups of adults who seem inevitably to have joined this type of festivity. This was almost certainly a consideration since the peace of the bishop had been disturbed on at least one prior occasion during or following the boys' celebrations *"by the unbridled insolence of the mob following the same (boys) and the throng of dishonourable men flocking together"*.

Similar regulations were made to control the feasts held during this season by the cathedral clergy.

The Boy at London, had he been aware of the privileges afforded other Boy Bishops, might have been exceedingly jealous.

If the St Paul's Boy Bishop's festivities were closely circumscribed, the Boy Bishop in York had a far more interesting and profitable time. A York *Computus* of 1396 [4] which seems to have been written by Nicholas of Newark, who had been appointed as guardian to the Boy Bishop's property, gives a detailed account. People of every class welcomed the chance to celebrate and in the absence of theatres as we know them, and other such places of entertainment, these celebrations often took place outside in the streets and market places. In winter, the opportunities for such open air activities were limited but there was still the chance to see a colourful procession. And so it was that in York and in many other places the Boy Bishop was not simply offered carefully supervised entertainment within the walls of the cathedral precinct, but was indulged with processions and visitations to abbeys, priories and the houses of great men. It can only be imagined what a release the York visitations would have been for the boys who, like other schoolboys, were confined in the schoolroom or church for almost all of their waking hours. John Cave, the Boy Bishop, was also the recipient of many valuable gifts and a substantial sum of money, although he probably did not handle much of the money himself since Nicholas was given that responsibility. As we have seen in the organisation of the election at York, the shrewd canons of that cathedral seem to have been endowed with a practical sense. The cathedral chapter might take inordinate care to ensure that the Boy Bishop had an unforgettable reign, but he was not allowed to fall prey to boyish extravagance nor be given the chance to lose the money. With long experience of caring for boys, they had adopted the attitude of benevolent control.

It is interesting to enquire into the nature of this visitation. Obviously it was not undertaken to defray the expenses of the Boy Bishop ceremonies in York, for the amounts raised from within the city more than covered these costs, and neither was it the case that the cathedral clergy saw the exercise as financially expedient for themselves or the Minster[5], as they received none of the money. Although the Boy Bishop received a generous sum when all expenses were paid, most of the money went on equipping the entourage and paying the other associated costs, and so the visitation, in the end, did not provide a vast source of wealth for him. It seems very likely that the chapter believed that such a visitation would provide a reward for a boy's good service, especially since at York, as we have seen, the Boy Bishop had to have given long and faithful devotion to the cathedral before he could be elected. It is perhaps also possible to view the visitation as a mirror of a true bishop's visitation by which means a prelate would monitor and control his clergy, although there were differences, since the Boy Bishop made visits to non-religious as well as to religious institutions, and to monasteries that would usually have been beyond the pastoral control of a diocesan bishop. But then we should not take the parallel with true bishops too far. No doubt there was an element of aping a bishop's pastoral visitation and there is evidence from Padua that the diocesan bishop was questioned about his stewardship of the Church, but obviously the boy would have little or no insight into the behaviour of the diocesan clergy, and no authority to do anything about them even if he did. Nevertheless his hosts were under an obligation to provide appropriate hospitality. As will be noticed later in looking at Le Mans and Padua, there could be strict penalties for refusing hospitality or tribute, or as at Toul for failing to arrange the ceremonies properly. Although not explicitly noted at York, it seems that generally the arrangement existed within a loosely-formalised framework. Generous hosts would be rewarded by the Boy Bishop's prayers, while others showing a meaner spirit might suffer sanctions. Both religious and secular houses appear to have been required to show the Boy Bishop a respect similar to that due to the true bishop.

The receipts from the Minster and City of York in 1396 were certainly substantial (Tables 1 and 2).

Table 1

From the Cathedral	£	s	d	a silver spoon, silver ring, silk purse
Christmas Day offerings		1	0	
Offerings on Holy Innocents	1	4	1	
Precentor		1	8	
Chancellor		2	0	
Treasurer		6	8	
Archdeacon of Richmond		6	8	
Nicholas de Feriby		6	8	
Thomas de Wallworth		6	8	
Total	2	15	5	

Table 2

From the City	£	s	d	
Abbot of St Mary's		6	8	
Archdeacon of the East Riding		3	4	
Total		10	0	

However, the receipts from the visitation outside the city were even greater, a total of £5 10s 0d, as will be seen later. This gave a grand total of £8 15s 5d. To put this sum into context it is worth remembering that a master mason or a lawyer could be expected to earn £10-£17 per year.[6]

Nonetheless, all this money was not destined to find its way into the boy's purse, for he was expected to pay the expenses of his visitation. On 23rd December a penny was spent on bread and 6d for ale. The Boy Bishop's great feast cost 15s 6½d, not to mention 6d for the cook's wages, and included some sumptuous fare (Table 3).

Table 3

The Great Feast	
Bread	46 field fares
Lord's bread	Small birds
Ale	Wine
Veal	Spices
Mutton	60 pears
Sausages	Honey
Two ducks	Mustard
Twelve chickens	Flour
Eight woodcocks	2 pounds of candles
A plover	Fuel

This was indeed a feast and contrasts markedly with what we know about the meagre and restricted diet of most medieval people. Soon there was further expenditure: 1s 4d for the supper on Holy Innocents' day itself which included bread, ale, veal, mutton, pepper and saffron.

Meanwhile, it was important to prepare carefully for the visitations, for it was of little use thinking merely in terms of a carefree romp through the countryside. Journeying over 280 miles[7] would naturally present problems that had to be surmounted; and then there were the dangers of the road to be taken into account. Thus, the practicalities of the boy's visitation had to be addressed, with safety and comfort as the priorities, and so a number of expensive purchases were made (Table 4).

Table 4

Purchases for travelling		
A torch weighing twelve pounds	4s	3d
A cap		9d
A pair of knives	1s	2d
A pair of spurs		5d
Lamb's wool for the Boy Bishop's overcoat	2s	6d
Furs	6s	0d
Faggots throughout the whole time		8d
Sea coal		7d
Charcoal		10d
28 Pairs of gloves for vicars[8] and masters of the schools	3s	4½d

The ceremonial purpose was not forgotten either and so some items were paid for on the Boy's behalf (Table 5)

Table 5

Purchases made on the Boy's behalf		
A pair of linen gloves		3d
A pair of sleeves or cuffs		3d
The Boy Bishop's gown		6d
A Paris candle	1s	4½d
Repairs to a silk cope		2d

Clearly this was a well-organised operation, probably made easier with years of practice.

After the supper on Holy Innocents' Day, there was a period of rest giving the organisers the chance to make sure that all the preparations were in order. It is not that travelling was unusual, for despite the lack of public transport, many people did make frequent journeys; it is the relative lack of safety that must be considered. Even in the fourteenth century the possibility of attack could not be ignored, although numbers usually provided sufficient protection. The roads, which in summer were little more than hard rutted tracks, in winter either became frozen solid or turned into beds of churned mud, never easy to negotiate. Thus it was rare in winter for riders to cover more than about twenty miles a day.

The first visitation was made on the octave day of Holy Innocents. The Boy Bishop and his entourage set out for Kexby, a mere seven mile journey. Here they were entertained by Sir Thomas Utrecht who gave the Boy Bishop half a noble (3s 4d).[9] The company then returned to a supper of bread, ale and meat, costing 11d.

The longest visitation took place three days later beginning on Sunday, 7th January and lasting fourteen days with a short return to York and then a further visitation of six days, completing the whole round on 27th January, though it seems that the boy might not have been expected to return to his studies until 2nd February. These journeys would not only bring in large sums of money, together with some valuable gifts, but would also allow the travellers to sample the hospitality of monasteries and great houses where they would be feasted and entertained. This was perhaps the closest the Boy Bishop would come to enjoying a holiday in the more modern sense of the word.

A breakfast of bread, meat and ale, costing 10d was served to the members of the party before they left, and 2d was paid for *"horse bread"*. The Boy Bishop had to be equipped with a new girdle (3d) and not long after the journey began his cap needed to be replaced (1d). The boy first paid a visit to the Prior of Kirkham and received 2s. The next stop at the Priory of Malton was more lucrative, the prior donating a noble (6s 8d) and then they pressed on to Leaconfield where the Countess of Northumberland was in residence. This was a visit well worth making, for she proved to be the most generous host of all, donating £1 and a gold ring. At Bridlington he received a noble from the prior and then half a noble from the Prior of Watton and the Rector of Baynton alike. When the procession passed through Beverley a new girth was required (1d) before they were able to proceed to the Priory of Meaux, where he received half a noble again. At Ferriby he was given 1s 8d, Sir Stephen de Scrope donated a noble and the Priory of Drax 2s 0d. The Abbey of Selby contributed a noble, the Prior of Pontefract half a noble, the Prior of St Oswald at Nostell a noble, the Prior of Monk Bretton half a noble and John

Depdene a further noble. From there they made their way to Lady Marmion at Tanfield where he was given another gold ring, another silk purse and a noble. Lady Darcy added half a noble and Lady Roos at Helmsley Castle another noble. The Abbeys of Rievaulx and Byland, and Newburgh Priory contributed a disappointing 2s each, with Marton Priory adding only 1s 8d, but then they probably had their own Boy Bishops to support and might well have been reluctant to donate to a Boy Bishop from the Minster. In view of the amount of money being collected it is clear that some provision must have been made for the security of the party, lest they fall prey to robbers. Saturday saw the Boy Bishop return with his company to York where they dined on fish, bread and ale.

Of course, there were significant costs incurred in making such a journey: the expense of keeping a mounted company in good order; money laid out for food and drink, when it was not possible to claim hospitality; money paid to attendants and ministers, and the giving of alms and other offerings; and finally the outlay for vestments and adornments (Table 6).

Table 6

Keeping the company in good order
New girth
Repair of old girth
Two horse combs
Ferries
Horse bread bought at Selby
Barber at Selby (probably for the men's beards)
Re-shoeing horses on three occasions
Hay and oats for the horses
Horse bread and hay
Cost of horses
Saddle

These expenses remind us that on such an expedition horses need constant care and attention, that it is not simply a case of mounting a horse in the morning and taking it to a stable at night. Accordingly provision had to be made for replacing tackle and for feed. There was not a large sum spent on provisions, since most food and drink was provided by the houses and monasteries where they stayed (Table 7).

Table 7

Food and drink
Food and drink
Wine for the Boy Bishop(probably his treat alone)

The identification of different voice parts in the accounts probably indicates not only that the company themselves provided some entertainment for their hosts but that they sang in different parts. There was a fair number of people required to organise the visitations, and the relative rates of remuneration are quite instructive, as Table 8 shows.

Table 8

Payments to attendants and ministers, and alms and offerings	£	s	d
Nicholas Newsome (tenor)		13	4
Robert Daltry (Newsome's steward)		6	8
Payments for preaching		2	1½
John Baynton (medius voice)		10	0
John Green		5	0
John Ellay		3	4
Succentor of the vicars		2	0
Subchancellor		1	0
Clerks to the vestments		1	0
Sacrists (to look after sacred vessels, etc.)		1	0
Master of the choristers		3	4
Common pence (possibly for choristers)		1	6
Offering (at Bridlington)			2
Alms (at Bridlington)			1
Total	2	10	6½

Then there were some further expenses (Table 9)

Table 9

Vestments and adornments	£	s	d
Wax for the boys (small candles/tapers)		1	0
Adornment of the episcopal chair			4
Wood for the stalls			4
Total		1	8

When the accounts were complete, £6 14s 10½d of expenses had to be set against the offerings of £8 15s 5d, giving the boy the handsome sum of £2 0s 6½d.

This visitation at York was by no means unique. It seems that by the time of John Cave the Boy Bishops had been engaged in such visitations of the diocese for many years. Twenty-seven years earlier, the master of choristers, John Gisson, had sworn on the sacred scriptures that he had faithfully handed over all the money due (£3 15s 1½d) to the Boy Bishop, Robert de Holme.[10]

In Hereford the Boy Bishop and his retinue were usually allowed a visitation of the local parishes on the day of Holy Innocents and a dinner provided by the chapter. The boy himself was often the recipient of monetary offerings, but on more than one occasion the chapter seems to have decided that there were more pressing needs than lining the boy's purse, such as providing education for the choristers.[11]

At Toul where, as we have already seen, the boys were permitted to place in the choir a representation of the canon organising the affair to mock him if he failed to do the job properly, there is also a record of the Boy Bishop's visitation.[12] On the morning of Holy Innocents' Day he rode in procession in great style, leading his companions across the town to the monasteries of St Mansuetus and St Aprus.[13] The canon was also expected to provide him with his horse, gloves and biretta. On arriving at the monasteries he sang an anthem and said a prayer. The monasteries in return gave him 18 Toul pennies, or if they could not afford this immediately he could accept a pledge of future payment or books. From this it is possible to gain a better idea of the customs of the Boy Bishop celebrations; they existed in many places not so much on the sufferance of adults, but because they were firmly established by right. At Toul money given was given rather as part of a recognised custom than because it was a voluntary donation, freely given (although indeed the donors might well feel happy to give it). The boy received his dues by virtue of his office and as remuneration for his singing and praying. All of this seems to illustrate how firmly the celebrations were built into the fabric of the Christmas period.

After Vespers the Boy Bishop and choristers ventured out into the streets once more, this time with music and farses (probably irreverent songs) along the usual processional route for an evening celebration. It was at supper on this day when the boys would stand in judgement over the canon, deciding whether he had provided a sufficiently good celebration.

The day following Holy Innocents' Day, after lunch, the boys were again on the streets in costumes disguising their appearances, where, weather permitting, farses were performed once more and perhaps miracle or morality plays, too. The entertainments were, however, meant to be decent. That evening the organising canon had once more to provide supper for the boys, but this time, no doubt to his relief that this would not lighten his purse further, he could use the left-overs from the previous night.

On the octave of the Holy Innocents the bishop in his grand robes of office went with his companions to the church of St Genevieve where, having sung the canticle for the Virgin herself together with the collect, he went to the parish house where they were provided with cake, apples, nuts and other types of food, and there the officers were appointed to correct the defects and excesses committed in the divine office during the whole of the following year. Any fines collected resulting from these offences would be used to pay the expenses of the ceremonies next year, apart from those expenses already assigned to the organising canon.[14] One can but sympathise with this canon, for having been elected by being presented with the rosemary cap, he was bound to use his own money for a magnificent supper and to provide a horse and other clothes for the Boy Bishop. He was responsible for all the arrangements; and what is more, if things went wrong, he could be subjected to humiliation and loss of his income, apparently on the whim of the boys.

A further case serves to emphasise the importance given to the rights exercised by the Boy Bishop. The Abbot of Beaulieu disputed the right of the Boy Bishop to claim hospitality as a right, saying giving such hospitality was merely an act of goodwill. The chapter of Le Mans disagreed and held that it was a duty that the Abbot must observe.[15]

In Laon there is a record of processions through the town in 1284 and 1397.[16] In 1454 four livres parsis were given to celebrate the feast, and the canons who assisted at the supper of the Boy Bishop in 1458 were each given twelve derniers parsis. In 1460 the Boy Bishop himself received sixty livres on St Nicholas's Day, the day of his election. Canon Jacques Cannet in 1527 bequeathed in his will 40 sols tournois to meet the expenses and cost of the Boy Bishop on the condition that he sang one anthem and one *De profundis* after the festive supper. There must have been a problem in 1490, because on 15th December the Patriarch of Fools and the Boy Bishop presented a petition to gain the chapter's permission to hold their respective feasts and to receive their gifts. The Boy Bishop was allowed to celebrate his feast but dressed in sober robes. Yet, for reasons known to himself, the Patriarch was permitted a feast only and with the threat of prison if he invited anyone to disrupt the proceedings. In fact, the trouble was to be expected at the adult Patriarch's celebrations, and in 1518 Albert Gossuin, a chaplain, was imprisoned for eight days for throwing down the light from the high gate above where the Patriarch was celebrating. In 1580 there is evidence of the chapter granting permission for the Boy Bishop ceremonies and donating 30 sols.[17] It seems that at that time it was customary for some fooling about to take place during the Mass on St Eloi's Day when the boy was elected. There was also another Boy Bishop elected by the pupils of the city whom the chapter were keen should not be confused with the cathedral's own Boy Bishop.

In Germany, it appears that not everything was as well ordered and dignified as at St Gall. In cathedrals and schools the pupils were given greater licence than in the monasteries and their behaviour began to cause great offence.[18] The innocent festivities of the feast had been supplanted by a more disruptive type of behaviour. Once released from the fear of punishment, the boys, led by the Boy Bishop or *"school-king"*, indulged in feasting, drinking bouts and boorish behaviour which included failing to pay any respect to schoolmasters and mocking their work. At Salisbury, Paris and London, to mention only some of the places we have already seen, it was the men who were the cause of most of the problems, and so in Germany, where they also claimed the same immunity from punishment as the boys, they were also blamed for the degeneration of the feast into something more disreputable. Here then there is a blurring of the distinction between the ceremonies of the Boy Bishop and its more notorious cousin, the Feast of Fools, about which more later.

Not everywhere was implicated. The ceremonies at Erfurt, for example, seem to have retained their original character. Nicholas Bibera in his satirical poem written in the thirteenth century describes a visitation where, according to the custom, the elected boy who led the pranks had to beg for gifts at the abbot's door.

> *Servant of Jesus, you too were once a child.*
> *You were then playing with your masters, just as those present are doing now.*
> *Then you enjoyed childlike fun – today you have dedicated your life to God.*
> *Don't let it displease you or make you angry if you become one of us.*
> *You are a child because of the child-like way within you.*
> *You were then a child because of your age, but now you are a child because of your simple ways.*
> *You are thus asked to give the boys small gifts.*
> *Are you thinking of giving some eggs? But who could satisfy the boys with eggs, Lord!*
> *Anything else would be more acceptable.*
> *If you are not short of money, we should be grateful for a mark or a coin.*
> *If, however, this seems too much and you refuse because of your thrift,*
> *Something else will do and you will gain your reward in heaven.*

The appeal to the "child-within" seems almost modern, and the complex persuasive pattern perhaps owes more to the artistic invention of the poet than to the children, but if the boys did put on some sort of performance in order to elicit gifts from the abbot then it parallels quite closely the more formal visitations of the Boy Bishop.

At Mainz,[19] between the time of election before the feast of St Nicholas and his installation on the feast of Holy Innocents, the Boy visited the Elector with a full complement of master canons and *"the rest of the nobility"* where they sang the hymn:

> *Now the youth in solemn manner recalls thy feast, abundant Nicholas, to express thy unworthy praises, priests' king.*
>
> *How great a noble example of piety and of a pure life didst thou, a boy, give to boys; nothing ignoble will please thee.*
>
> *Therefore thy youthful children, lo! stand before thee rightly, summit of thy people, a gathering, and equally the senate of priests celebrates thee duly.*

As elsewhere, the singing of the hymn was the token price for an invitation to a banquet. In addition, the schoolmaster or preceptor was given a gift of money to help to pay for the expenses of the celebration. Three commonly held beliefs – that the chapter had often wished to abolish the custom but lacked the authority; that should an Elector die during the Boy Bishop's reign he should enjoy the electoral income until the election of a new elector; that on the death of a vicar of the cathedral the Boy Bishop would receive his income – all seem to be false.

At Padua, on the eve of Holy Innocents, the Boy Bishop in full pontifical rig of cope and mitre, preceded by incense and candles, went in procession with his entourage to the bishop's palace.[20] At the entrance he sang the antiphon *Suffer the little children* before being censed. Having entered the palace, the Boy Bishop, the adult bishop, the clerks and scholars and even any laymen who happened to be present all sat down while the boy questioned the bishop to ascertain whether or not he had been a good steward over the goods of the Church during the past year, along with many other types of jesting. It is not possible to determine whether this was a genuine interrogation by the boy from a child's perspective, whether the boy merely repeated questions given to him by an adult, or whether it was a gentle piece of play-acting. The presence of so many people might argue for its more serious purpose, while the jests that followed perhaps indicate the opposite. After that was finished, the evening took on a much more celebratory note as the Boy Bishop called for wine to be served to everyone.

On Holy Innocents' Day itself, the duties of host fell on the shoulders of the Boy Bishop. He extended his hospitality to all the clerks, canons and scholars wanting to dine with him in the guesthouse. After dinner, vested in cope, mitre and gloves, and with the episcopal ring on his finger, he set off on horseback with his chaplains, also in copes, and the scholars and canons of his household to bless the men and women of the town and to visit the monasteries tributary to the cathedral. These included the monasteries of St Justin, St Stephen, St Sophia, St Leonard and St Peter. The company would dismount where the Boy Bishop directed and they would be received with honour, being formally greeted, as a real bishop would be, by abbots, priors, abbesses, monks and nuns, bearing incense and holy water. They processed into the church where the Boy Bishop, having prostrated himself before the altar in prayer, turned to offer a blessing to all present. The religious side completed, they all entered the cloister where everyone drank the wine ordered by the Boy Bishop. However, any monastery refusing to pay the accustomed tribute would be placed under a ban and the true bishop approaching in solemn procession, with priest and people singing litanies, would refuse to enter the monastery. The ban would remain in force until the monastery had made amends to the Boy Bishop.

Where there were significant sums of money at stake, it is to be expected that disputes would arise over territory, as was sometimes the case in our more recent history between competing carol-singing choirs. The Boy Bishop at Ottery St Mary was forbidden in Bishop Grandisson's statutes from making processions outside Ottery, quite possibly on account of disputes with a neighbouring parish.[21]

The accounts of Finchale Priory near Durham contain a list of payments made to the Boy Bishop (Table 10).[22] The first mention is in 1367 when it is included in other sums. This continued to be the case until 1395 when it appears as a separate item. After 1395, it is not possible to say whether in the years the payment does not appear it was because it was not paid, or because it was again accounted for in a another way. There are also payments to cover the costs of required writing materials.

From 1449 onwards it seems likely that all the payments went to the Boy Bishop at Durham.

For two years at least (1423 and 1434) Elvetham, a manor of Finchale Priory, had its own Boy Bishop who was the recipient of 1s 8d.

The feast centred on St Nicholas's Day in Bristol, which is perhaps the older date for the celebration and not just for the election; or perhaps here it was simply because the church's dedication was St Nicholas. After Mass and dinner, the mayor, sheriff and their company assembled at the mayor's counter to await the arrival of the Boy Bishop, playing dice (which the town clerk had to find).[23] The Boy Bishop with his company then sang to them and gave his blessing before being served with bread and wine. The festivities concluded with the company returning to church to hear Evensong.

Hyde Abbey and St Swithin's Priory in Winchester both held the Boy Bishop's feast. At St Swithin's the Boy received gifts of wine and beer to be drunk at the supper, as well as gifts from those holding important offices.[24] Once again the boyish desire to dress up, perform, show off and have fun was indulged by the master of St Swithin's. The boys, joining those of St Elizabeth's Chapel, must have gained much enjoyment from putting on girls' clothes and going to the convent of the Blessed Virgin on Holy Innocents' Day to dance, sing and sport before the nuns. Similarly the boys at Hyde were furnished with masks and dresses for their visit to the bishop at Wolvesey Palace, the constable of Winchester Castle and all the monasteries of the City of Winchester.

Table 10

Finchale Abbey – payments to the Boy Bishop		
1395	3s 4d	
1413	3s 4d	It is made clear here that it is not a payment by right
1414 -1422	3s 4d	It seems each year
1423	3s 0d	The monks also gave 1s 8d to a Boy Bishop of Elvett
1424 -1429	3s 4d	Each year
1430 -1436	2s 0d	Each year
1439 -1446	2s 0d	Each year
1447	9s 3d	Includes other donations
1448	14s 4d	Includes other donations
1449	12s 6d	For the Boy Bishop and choir at Christmas, and other gifts.
1457	£1 6s 0d	There may have been payments in the intervening years
1458		It appears the payment was withdrawn
1466 -1528	3s 4d	The payments continue with some gaps until 1528, the last of the account rolls.

The fifth Earl of Northumberland showed generosity towards the Boy Bishops with an annual gift to them of a noble, and even if he were not able to attend his chapel on Saint Nicholas's Day he allowed a payment of half a noble to be made if St Nicholas *"com owte of the towne where my lord lyeth"*.[25] He showed similar generosity to the Boy Bishops of York and Beverley.[26]

> *My lord usith and accustimyth yerely when his lordship is at home*
> *to yef unto the Barne-Bishop (Boy Bishop) of Beverlay when he*
> *comith to my Lorde in Christmas Hally-Dayes when my Lord kepith*
> *his Hous at Lekynfeld – xx s. (£1)*

> *My lord usith and accustimyth yerely when his lordship is at home*
> *to yef unto the Barne-Bishop of Yorke when comes over to my Lord*
> *in Chrisynmase-Hally-Dayes as he is accustomed yerely – xx s.*

Clearly, the Earl had a soft-spot for the institution of the Boy Bishop.

The celebrations at Senlis were not confined to the cathedral either, for they continued at the college of St Rieul where it seems that eight sols were given to the vicars for the customary ceremonies.[27]

Although there is some variation in the gifts offered, money, food and entertainment feature frequently. There is a mention of the Archbishop of Vienne who by ancient custom was required to give the Boy Bishop (Bishop of the Innocents), elected on 15th December, some money, a measure of wine and some wood. The boy also received wood from each canon.[28] The cathedral at Amiens in 1533 set aside 60 sous for the ancient Boy Bishop celebrations.[29] In Péronne the chapter paid for the lunch and dinner on the eve of Holy Innocents and in 1563 they also paid for the dinner on Holy Innocents itself.[30] While in 1592 the choir received wheat and 25 silver sous, the Boy Bishop's gift was at the discretion and generosity of the true bishop. The Boy Bishop in Noyon received 40 sous parsis and four bushels of wheat in 1419, and in 1497 the Boy Bishop approached the chapter to require that the dean supply white bread (the most expensive type); three kinds of wine: red, white and claret; and other customary things such as dragees and fruit.[31] The importance attached to the rights of the Boy Bishop is illustrated here. The Boy Bishop petitioned the chancellor to prohibit the church of St Martin's establishing a Boy Bishop on the grounds that this would trespass on his rights.[32] Again in 1527 there is a record that the chapter consented to the election of a Boy Bishop but they would not allow the ceremonies themselves. At the Monastery of St Quentin the boy abbot was given a pair of gloves.[33] The Boy Bishop also went visiting in Cartagena.

The costs, however, could be high. Sometimes, as at Corbie, it was hard to find the money to pay for the celebrations. Here a monk was obliged to sell a house on behalf of the abbey in order to meet the expenses of the feast and a morality play.[34]

At Rheims any who wanted to enjoy the feast had to make a contribution which was recorded carefully by a clerk. In 1479 the chapter undertook to pay the expenses but the celebrations had to be without masks, the sounds of trumpets or riding through the town.[35] It seems that at Sens the amount the chapter could afford for the choristers depended upon their fluctuating income. At one time the choristers were given a grant of wine and rights in the chapter woods as well as some dues from the local market. But the chapter replaced the market rights with a small income.[36] However, at Liege the expenses were not borne by the chapter but by the last canon appointed.

There was a short visitation of a different type allowed to the Boy Bishop in Tours. Here he was first installed in the convent at Beaumont where he received all the young clerics who came to see him on the day before Holy Innocents. In this church he was raised on a throne and robed in his vestments. After the boys' cantor had intoned the responsory *Sancta* at the great door and the anthem *Alma* with *Gloria* before the altar of the Blessed Virgin, the Boy Bishop, having blessed the nuns, rode back to Tours where, after being installed in the cathedral on a throne before the treasurer's door, the services seem to have proceeded in the usual way.[37]

Sad to relate, as we have already seen at Paris and Salisbury (Chapter 1), not every visitation ended happily.

Perhaps it is because we are accustomed to filter the customs of the Middle Ages through the glass of our historical imagination that we are liable to colour the Boy Bishops' soliciting of money and entertainment with prettier hues than we allow the activities of contemporary childish activities such as "trick-or treat", which is often dismissed as a brash import, if not almost the crime of demanding money with menaces. Nevertheless, it is likely that we shall make a distinction between the well-scrubbed boy dressed as a bishop "singing for his (albeit expensive) supper" and the gang of grinning demons brazenly demanding treats.

6

The Sermon

It was all well and good for the medieval clergyman to extol the virtues of boyish innocence as he paraded his carefully prepared Boy Bishop before the people of the cathedral, but in reality those clergymen and schoolmasters who had daily dealings with boys would have nursed no illusions about their innocence. They would have experienced at first hand that they were often boisterous, loud, coarse, violent, disrespectful, inattentive, lazy, greedy and in need of constant correction. If the boys were in truth paragons, then there would have been little need of the type of sermon that was preached. No doubt, the boys showed a virtuous side to their characters, too, but the countless number of improving texts written in that period – the increasing rate of literacy making them more generally accessible – aimed at inculcating good behaviour in boys argues a widely-held acceptance of the need for reform. The moralists of the time continually worried about the behaviour of children and adolescents.

The constant tension between the ideal of childish innocence – the result of adult optimism – and annoyance or despair at the behaviour of real children is one that figures quite prominently in these sermons. There can be seen in many historical periods a perception among adults that children in the past were somehow better behaved, more moral, more hardworking and more respectful than those of the present. Paradoxically, in addition to the injunction to adults to become more like innocent children, the sermons, building on the centuries-long tradition of preaching on the Holy Innocents, represent to some extent at least a desire to reform the seemingly poor behaviour of the contemporary young.

The three sermons[1] that have come down to us are certainly moralising in tone and that it is to be expected since they were written not by the boys themselves but by clergymen, one of whom, Erasmus, also wrote a book about proper behaviour in society.[2] Whether or not it was the unvarying practice that the boys preached a sermon prepared by adults, it seems likely that the clergy would have wanted control over what the boy might say. The potential for embarrassment and disaster would surely have been too great to allow the Boy Bishop to construct his own sermon, although it might have given us some interesting insights into the mind and experience of the medieval child.

The Gloucester Sermon

The Gloucester sermon, written by Richard Ramsey, was preached in the cathedral by chorister John Stubs on Holy Innocents' Day, 1558. Richard Ramsey had been awarded his BA in 1539, became Vicar of Wellan in 1546, Rector of Shenington in 1555 and was at one time a canon of the cathedral.[3] This is a virtuoso piece – to be delivered by a boy who must have had a talent for oratory – by turns: daring, challenging, cruel, critical, mocking, self-deprecating, witty, funny, finely constructed and yet with the serious purpose of persuading people to see the importance of innocence on the path to salvation.

As was usual, the boy prefaces the sermon with a biblical quotation, in this case:

> *"Nisi conversi fueritis, et efficiamini sicut parvuli, non intrabitis in regnum celorum"* (*Unless you are converted and become like little children you shall not enter the kingdom of heaven*).[4]

The sermon commences in quite a startling way. One might expect that a boy preaching in the cathedral, not only before his peers but before adults as well, might begin by adopting a fairly apologetic tone, asking them to pardon his presumptuousness in seeking to instruct them; but he immediately adopts an aggressive and monitory stance instructing the adults and adolescents alike that Christ's warning to become like little children is to be taken very seriously indeed, if they wish to enter the kingdom of heaven.

> *Among all the conclusions in holy Scriptures, which are many and marvellous, Ryght worshypfull audience, this is not the lest to be marvellyd at, doubtyd and dreadyd of all yow that are no[t] childer, but men, women, and yonggolds, of years and discretion* [5]

He then launches an attack on the Protestant literalists who were more concerned with a literal reading of Scripture than its true meaning. He points that out the literalists face the same problem as Nicodemus who was perplexed by Christ's teaching about having to be reborn.[6] But the Boy argues that Christ set himself against such literalist interpretations by explaining that there was no expectation of a physical change, only a spiritual one.

> *...yow specially whych alow no construction of the Scriptures but only the letter as it lyeth...*

> *Now to yow that hange of the letter and not of the sprite [spirit], this change, for a great one to be changed into a lytill one, and an old man to becum a babe agayne, may seme no less strange and impossible to yow than dyd the mystery of regeneracion, or new birth, unto Nichodemus, when he said unto Christ... "How kan a man be born when he is ones [once] old? Is it possible for hym to torne into his mother's womb agayne, and so be borne anew, and becum of an old man a child agayne?"... But our Saviour Christ gave hym to understand eare [before] he went, that there was a birth spirituall in water and in the Holy Ghost...*

In the same way the requirement to become like little children does not mean a physical transformation, but a conversion of the heart.

> *In lyke maner understand yow this conclusion of our Saviour, not as the letter soundeth, by a miraculous or monstruose conversion of a man in to child as touching age, stature and discretion, but of a morall conversion...*

And this requires adults to adopt the virtues of children, rather than their physical form, because few adults are uncorrupted.

> *...it is possible ynough for the greatest of men to becum as litill childer, and for the eldest of women to becum in the lyknes and maners as young babes, which are symple, without gyle, innocent and wythowt harme, and all pure wythowt corruption, as few above the age of childer are...*

The presentation of this material is startling enough. No doubt the adults would by this time be listening very carefully, some fairly indignantly, as was the intention. It is an unusual adult who welcomes criticism from children, especially at that time since many adults viewed the behaviour of the young with much suspicion. However, the sermon certainly did not avoid difficult or controversial topics. The boy then wonders how it could be that those being like children could enter heaven if, as Christ said, the kingdom of heaven was being seized by violence.[7] He explains that the violence needed to attain heaven is not, as one might imagine, performing violent acts but suffering acts of violence whether inflicted by another or inflicted on oneself. Thus, those who suffer from the violence of others, he believes, have "used" violence. And those who have castrated themselves to avoid the consequences of lust; the apostles who followed Christ, renouncing the world and worldly goods; and any who give up evil and sinful living have used justifiable violence to gain the kingdom of heaven.

> *Such violence usyd thei, which utterly forsakyng the pleasures of the flesh, dyd castrate themselves for the kyngdom of heaven… Such violence usyd the Apostles which utterly renownsyd the world and all worldly goodes and folowyd Christ… and all other which, for the love of the kyngdom do willingly forsake their evill trade and synfull lyving, stryvyng with the world and with themselves to entre into the kyngdom.*

Even Christ himself, claims the boy, used violence to regain his own kingdom through his sufferings throughout his life.

> *"Dyd it not behove Christ to suffre as he dyd, and so entre into his own kyngdom?" He suffryd this violence not only on the crosse… but also in his cradell, and in his mother's armes in his childhode and infancy, when kyng Herod conspiryd his death.*

Having firmly established that the righteous who suffer violence are on course to enter heaven, he then makes his next important point. It was by the violence of Herod that the Holy Innocents gained the heavenly kingdom, being slain in the pursuit of Christ and dying in their innocence. Moreover, since they did not die simply for professing faith in Christ, but for his very person, they must be regarded as martyrs above all other martyrs. Yet the defining characteristic that gave them the glory of martyrdom was their innocence, for they suffered an undeserved fate; there can be no martyrdom if the suffering and death is justified

> *Yet thei that sawght Christes bloud, being uncerteyn of Christys*
> *person, dyd onmercifully spill the bloud of all the Innocentes that*
> *were about the age of Christ, from 2 years old and inward, by means*
> *whereof their death was and is imputed to them for acceptable*
> *martyrdom… And so every one of these Innocentes dyd shed their*
> *bloud, not only in the quarell of Christ [for Christ's sake], but also*
> *in the person of Christ, which was a prerogative above all other*
> *martyrs; for although many holy martyrs have dyed in the quarell of*
> *Christ, yet dyd never none but these blessyd Innocents dye for the*
> *person of Christ; and this is their prerogative in martyrdom, besides*
> *the rightuosness of their most pure innocency, withowt the which the*
> *suffryng of ther bloud shed and their quarell for Christ cold not gyve*
> *them the glory of martyrdom, for a malefactor that suffreth not*
> *innocently, but for his own gilt and deservyng, is worthy that he*
> *suffreth…and to loke for no thankes of God at all.*

There is this continued emphasis on innocence, in part because the cause of the
Holy Innocents had both bothered and intrigued the medieval churchmen. On the
one hand they debated how unbaptised children before the age of reason could be
worthy of entering Heaven if they had not actually made any decisions or
performed any deeds to deserve such a reward; and on the other they were
fascinated and appalled by the brutality directed at such young children. However,
as is plain from this sermon, these victims of Herod had been enrolled at the top of
the list of martyrs, setting a spiritual pattern for the whole of Christendom which
was enjoined to emulate their innocence. The writer of the sermon was determined
to make sure that his audience understood this and he continued in the same vein:

> *…innocency…as I said, is a vertue most necessary: so necessary that*
> *withowt it ther is no perfitt charity [love], withowt the which no*
> *cause, no payne, no pacience, no quarell, no, not the quarrel of faith*
> *and Christ, avayleth or profiteth to the title of martyrdom, or to the*
> *title of the kyngdom.*

To make sure that the point had been fully comprehended the boy quotes the
examples of Abel,[8] the Holy Innocents again and St Stephen, to show that a
requirement of true martyrdom is innocence.

The point about the requirement for innocence being made, the boy requests that those listening join him in prayer – as was customary at this point – so that grace may be given to him to expound his points well, and that they may be given the grace to heed his words and follow them for their own salvation. In his prayer he requests God's help, pleading rather disingenuously that since he is but a child he lacks adult eloquence to sway the minds of adults and children to hold fast to virtue. In fact, this is a beautifully written passage, and the irony would not be lost on the audience that in his confession of lack of eloquence he is at his most eloquent.

> *...I am but a child, not only as Jeremye [9] was, but I am a child in dede; but if I were a man that had utterance and eloquence to set forth and prosecute thi word, which I have begon with all in my theme towchyng the change of men into childer, Lord, how earnest I wold be with the elders of this audience to convert them selves and ther maners to the lykness of litill childer, that thei myght be suer of thy gloriose kyngdom. Lord, how fervent I wold be with my late companions, yong boys, which yet beare the name of childer to retagne and kepe the commendable virtues of childer and not to degenerate from their vertues, that I myght make them also partenars of thy kyngdom. But I am a very child in these matters and kan not speake halfe perfectly.*

Of course, this is more than a prayer. It is brilliant rhetoric and a pointed criticism of his listeners. While apparently addressing God, the boy insinuates to the adults that they are in need of reform, while at the same insisting to the children that they are duty-bound to keep their virtue. Then having driven home these points forcefully, he has the audacity at the end to claim again that he is only a child who lacks rhetorical ability. However, if any believed that this apparent deficiency would stop him from preaching at them, they were mistaken.

> *What then, good people? Because I kan not speake perfectly and eloquently shall I speake nothing at all?... Speake I must, allthough lyke a child and stammer owt of this word of God a briefe exhortacion to both sortes, the elders and yongers, as well as I kan.*

With this piece of self-deprecation clearly contradicted by his oratory, the audience must have been anticipating a strong line. They were not to be disappointed. The boy launches into a blistering attack on adults and youngsters alike. His observations are sharp, hard-hitting, witty and effective and he even has the ability to "play" his audience. Many there must have been squirming at the sheer ferocity of his attack. The execution is outstanding.

First of all he selects the adults, identifying their faults which are bluntly coupled with a stark warning.

> *...yow must nede reforme your corrupt maners, which are dissonant and disagreable... or else you kan not loke for the kyngdom of heaven...*

> *... the kyngdom of heavyn wold not be gotten by pride, ambition, contencion, envy, emulacion, stowtness and elacion...*

Although they are to be as children in spirit, they are not to emulate them in lack of *"wit"* and understanding. In a clear reference to the new Protestantism he warns them not to *"be still as childer that be wavering and wilbe caried hyder and thyder with every blast of doctrine"*, for it is *"lak of witt if he [a Christian man] be caried from the doctrine of his awncient relligion in to a new fanglyd doctrine that has no suertiey in it, but is inconstant as the wynd"*.

The corruption of adults is to be contrasted with the virtues of children.

> *Considre well the nature of innocent childer, and yow shall perceive in them no maner of malice, no envy, no disdayne, no hurtfullness, no synfull affection, no pride, no ambition, no singularitie, no desyre of honor, of riches, of carnalitie, of revenginge, or quitting, evyll for evyll; but all the affections quiet, in all pacience, in all simplicitie, in all puritie, in all tractableness, in all obedience, in all humilitie, and in all innocency; and no such synfull affections reigning in them as commynly rageth in men and women of years.*

He further explains that innocence provides half of what is required: doing good is the other. By implication the adults fall short. The children listening to this, if they were honest, might not quite have recognised all these virtues in themselves, but it was an occasion for feeling very smug indeed while the adults suffered under the verbal lash.

The Boy Bishop then turns his attention to the children and their smugness was to be short-lived, for they were to be his next focus of attack.

He begins slowly, building to a climax. First he warns the children *"not to learn the vices and evill qualities"* of their elders, but then the onslaught commences. He says that he is telling them not to emulate the sins of their elders not so much because they are more virtuous than their elders, but rather because they are falling into these same sins at an earlier and earlier age and need a stern corrective.

> *And tyme it is to call upon yow this to do, for not only I, but the world, do se in yow that yow and the very litill ones that follow yow do grow nowadayes so fast owt of this innocent state that it is wonder to me to se amonge yow so many childer in years and so few innocentes in maners.*

Once begun, he quickly warms to his theme, explaining, in a way that will probably not be that unfamiliar to us, that 7 year olds lack the innocence that used to be found in 14 year olds and even three year olds are worse than 9 or 10 year olds used to be.

> *I am not very old my selfe to speake by experience; but I have hard say of my elders that a child was wont to continew an innocent untill he was 7 years old, and untill 14 years he was provyd to be of such vertue and honest nurture that he deservyd the love and prayse of all people; and now we shall not fynd such a one at 7 as was then at 14, nor at 5 as was then at 7, nor scant at 3 as was then at 9 or 10 years old.*

If the adults had thought the language used about them was harsh and pointed, there is still worse for the children to endure. There could be no vestige of smug superiority left among them by this point.

> *Tell me, yow boys, yow childer, you litill ones, are yow not ashamyd of your partes that yow are so sone corruptyd? so sone ripe, and so sone rottyn? so late innocentes, and so sone lewd lads? deservyng*

nother [neither] love nor prayse of any honest person. What yow are I kan not tell; but, a my honestie, I am both ashamyd of it and sory for it, that yow should so slandre the name of childer, and deceive your elders, which have an eye unto yow to note and folow your maners, as thei are advertysed by the wordes of Christ.

What must have been particularly galling about this attack – beside the marvellously pointed use of the orator's craft – the direct address, the rhetorical questions, the patterning and the balance – was the knowledge that he, a boy himself, seemed to be setting himself to judge them as though he lacked any such vices, something the boys would have known to be untrue, as the sermon makes clear later.

With such corruption all around, even among the children, the Boy Bishop feels that he ought to seek a boy who would be a good example to them all. And so begins the next stage of his rhetorical display as he mischievously seeks in vain among all the groups of boys for such an example. Firstly he wonders whether the boys of the city might be worth considering, but dismisses that idea very quickly as he describes their behaviour; even the youngest boy in the street is unworthy, for such boys are as sinful as adults. Perhaps, he thinks, the grammar schools might be a better option, being set up specifically to encourage learning and good behaviour; yet when the grammar school boys themselves are looked at it is clear that they provide very poor examples indeed. The next likely group is the boys of the song school. But since the Boy Bishop was recently one of their number he claims to know them very well indeed and gives sound reasons why their behaviour in church, apart form anything else, makes them completely unsuitable.

But wher shall I fynd them? In the citie? I dare not warrant yow to folowe the childer of the citie, no not the yongest of all, if thei be ones owt of ther mothers' handes and kan run abowt the streates and speake of all thinges perfittly; for thei have be scoyld at home that of them as yong as thei are yow may learne as evill properties as yow have already of your own; yea and perhapps the same which the child learnyd of yow before, as to swere with a grace, as som termes the othes that cum from the hart, with a stomake to curse bitterly, to blaspheme, to lye, to moke ther elders, to nykname ther aequalls, to knowledge no dutie to ther betters, and such other many mo[re]...

Which then? The childer that go to scole in the grammer scoles under a master? A man wold think yea [indeed], because thei are scoles set up purposly for the good educacion of childer, as well in good nurture as in good learning; but I dare not warrant yow to folow the childer of the grammer scoles, for, how so ever it happ, nurturyd thei are as evill or rather worse than the other... ripe and redy in all lewd libertie.

Which then? The queresters [choristers] and childer of the song-scole? Beware what yow do: for I have experience of them more than of the other. Yt is not so long sens I was one of them myself but I kan remember what shrewness was used among them, which I will not speake of now; but I kan not let this pass ontouched how boyyshly thei behave themselves in church, how rashly thei cum into the quere [choir] without any reverence, never knele not cowntenaunce to say any prayer or Pater noster, but rudely squat down on ther tayles and justle with ther felows for a place; a non they startes me owt of the quere agayne, and in agayne, and out agayne, and thus one after an other, I kan not tell how oft nor wherfor but only to gadd about and gas abrode, and so cum in agayne and crosse the quere fro one side to another and never rest, withowt any order, and never serve God nor our Lady with mattyns or with evynsong.

Having examined the various groups of boys in vain for an example, with a preacher's flourish, he turns to the children before him saying that they remind him of the story in which Christ set a child in front of the apostles in order to teach them the virtues of humility and innocence. One angelic looking little boy before him, he says, certainly looks like a child that might be set in the midst of them to provide a similar example of pure childhood, meekness and virtue. He clearly gives the appearance of innocence. But he is quickly damned with a devastating and unexpected warning.

Loke in his face and yow wold think that butter wold not melt in

> *his mouth; but as smothe as he lokes, I will not wysh yow to folow*
> *hym if you know as much as I do. Well, well! all is not gold that*
> *shynes, nor all are not innocent that beare the face of childer.*

At this point, despairing of finding any suitable examples among the children who have reached the age of discretion, he asks his audience to consider as examples of innocence those still under their mothers' control who have not yet learned to speak properly.

He now asks how it might be that with so many children to choose from there is such a small choice of good examples available. The answer is one that we too have heard all too frequently.

> *...where is the great falte? Evyn in you that are ther parentes, ther*
> *fathers, mothers and ther scolemasters.*

Following this identification of those he believes are blameworthy in allowing children to develop evil ways, he explains what is wrong with the way children are raised. Reading this, one is struck by how modern all of his complaints sound: over-indulgent parents who even when they hear the most foul language used by their offspring fail to discipline them; parents who seek to be loved by their children, who do not know the meaning of love and duty; fathers and mothers who in order to hear the child protest a preference for themselves over the other parent compete for the child's affections and dare do nothing to displease him; and parents who constantly pet and indulge children when they do not deserve it. This is in itself interesting, and a possible corrective to our worries about our children, but it also illustrates a particular attitude of mind. Although Philip Ariès's view that children in the Middle Ages were largely ignored has come in for harsh criticism in more recent years from historians such as Hanawalt[10] and Martindale[11] who believe that the children of that period were more likely to have been cherished by their parents than Ariès allowed, it is quite possible to argue that the attitude towards children had in fact gradually evolved and that this in no small part was owing to the influence of the Church, which, as we have seen, in the Boy Bishop ceremonies, placed constant emphasis on the central importance of the young. It is possible to go further and to suggest that so successful had the Church been in changing perceptions that, as this sermon demonstrates, parents had found themselves at the other extreme, becoming over-fond and over-indulgent of their children. The boy reiterates his condemnation of those charged with the children's upbringing.

Where is the great falte? Even in the parentes and, fathers, mothers and scolemasters, which do nother teach their childer good, nother chastice them when thei do evill; when thei lye and swere as I have hard some do, Good Lord, how abominably! and curse with plages and pestilence and murrens upon ther felows, brothers and sisters, evyn ther parentes standying by and hearing them; and yet not a word of correction… And what is the matter? a folysh affection and a fond [doting/foolish] opinion in the parentes which very fondly seke the love of ther child that knoweth not what love or dutye meaneth, that he might say "I am father's boy" or "I am mother's boy" and "I love father (mother) best"; to wyn this word, and the love of the child, the parentes contend who shall make the most of the child, and by these means no partye dare displease hym, say he or do he never so ongraciously, but both parties dandill hym and didill hym and pamper hym and stroke his hedd and sett hym a hye bence and gyve him the swetyst soppe in the dish evyn when he lest deserve it: this marrs the child, it makes hym to thynke he does well when he do stark nought.

The criticism is firmly aimed at the parents, yet the children would have cause to worry, for the Boy Bishop recommends that age-old remedy, endorsed by no lesser authority than King Solomon, famed for his wisdom.

Dyd you never here, yow fond mothers, what the wise Salomon [Solomon] saith Qui parcitur virgae odit filium, *"Thei that spare the rodd do hate the child."*

Many children would, no doubt, beg to differ. But the boy presses home his argument and asks quite sensibly where lies the good in mothers beating a cushion or a bench instead of a naughty child and then burning the rod, when the cushion or rod can have done no wrong. With straightforward logic he asks why the child does not feel the pain of punishment when he has been naughty. For those of a more sensitive turn of mind he explains that in any case the rod can do no harm to a child, for it breaks no bones – a fairly robust defence of the practice.

…it must nede be a fond love that you beare toward your childer in

> *this point, specially in such mothers as when ther children do a falt,*
> *and never so many faltes, which will not ones touch the child, but*
> *take the rod and beat the quyssion [cushion] or the forme [bench]*
> *and afters born [burn] the rodd and say thei spare not the rodd. O*
> *fond, fond mothers what falt have the quyssion don to be bettyn?*
> *what falt the rod don to be brent. Your child have done the fault,*
> *why do he not smart of the rodd? Why do yow spare the child? What*
> *hurt kan the rodd do to your child? Ys it not old and a tru saying*
> *"The rodd breakes no bones?"*

Fathers fare no better. He says that they often excuse their reluctance to use the rod by explaining that they do not want beat the courage out of their sons. That, however, is to miss the point completely: boys should be beaten so that they lack the courage to commit vice. Moreover, uncorrected boys will become so hardened in their bad ways that they will develop contempt for their fathers not being able to rule them. Failure to discipline sons is "to place a rod in pickle". Such is the reward of foolish tenderness.

> *The fathers are as fond agayne on the other part: "Nay (say thei) if*
> *I should beate my child and kepe hym undre and in awe now, I*
> *should kill his corage in his youth and take away his hart that he*
> *shall never be bold when he is a man. Mary! [12] that is the very thyng*
> *that is meanyd in all good educacion, to discorage youth utterly as*
> *touching vice and vicious matters and embolden and encourage*
> *them in all probity and virtue and virtuous maners. To lake a*
> *stomake and boldness in vice is no lake nor disprayse...but yf your*
> *desire be to have them stowt in evill demaner, yow shal be the first*
> *that shall have experience of that stowtness; for, after a litill time,*
> *thei wil be so styfe and stubborn against yow that yow shall not be*
> *able to rule them yf you wold, and, in conclusion, they will*
> *contempne yow and sett yow at nought above all other persons. This*
> *is the retorne of such fond tendreness.*

The schoolmasters are the next to receive his advice. They, he says, will have to account to God for how well they have taught their pupils and whereas parents fashion the child's body, a schoolmaster fashions his soul and can thus be accounted his third parent. He wants schoolmasters to bear down as rigorously on bad behaviour as they do on mistakes in language and music.

> *Allmyghtie God regardeth the litill ones, and wold not have them to be led from hym by yow, but by yow to be brought unto hym; and this he will require at your handes, as well as at the parentes, for your scole is your cure,[13] and yow shall give accomptess for every scoler in your scole for the tyme beyng…*

> *…as the carnall parentes by carnalitye do fascion the body, so the scolemaster do or owght to fascion the soule of the child by good educacion in learnying of good nurture and vertue; and therefore the scolemaster that so doth is cowntyd to be the 3rd parent to the child.*

> *Yow scholemasters have a good order in your scoles for breaking Priscian's [14] head or syngyng out of tune. I wold yow wold take the same order for breakyng of God's comandementes and ontunynge of Godes harpe.*

It is quite easy to feel that the parents, if they had not already taken his message to heart, would be feeling highly resentful, and it is almost possible to sense the clenching of boyish fists ready to teach the self-righteous traitor a well-deserved lesson of their own. However, in a final oratorical flourish the Boy Bishop makes a determined attempt to negate any ill-feeling by using the tactic of tackling potential criticism head on. He recognises that it might not sit well for a young boy to upbraid everyone sitting in front of him, but he excuses himself by saying that it cannot be a bad thing if everybody does amend their lives. To parry criticism of his speaking in this way he explains a number of things about himself. He says that those who knew him when he was younger know all about his boyish faults and he confesses that he was once as bad as most boys. With some wistfulness he says that he has paid for that and that he has now grown up, leaving behind all the shrewishness of his younger years. He concludes with the hope that all may be pure and innocent and so find entrance into the kingdom of heaven.

> *Perhaps some will think hert in ther myndes that I am very bold to*

fynd so many faltes with so many parties – fathers, mothers, scolemasters, childer, scolers, and no scollers; and take upon me to reforme my elders, I beyng so yong in age as I am, and to reprove others wherin I am not all clere my selfe, as some will judge that knew me in my childhode. Well! if we all amend we shalbe never the worse; and I confesse to them that I was sumtyme, as yet the most of them are, shrewd ynough for one, but I paid well for it, and have now left it; and I may alledge for my self the words of S Pawl... "When I was a chyldysh boy, my discrecion was therafter, my words and dedes were therafter; the fansys and desires of my hart were therafter; but now that I have cum to be a man, I have cast of all boy's touches",15 that is to say, all shrowdness of childhod, as I wold yow all had don, retayning the puritie of your childhod, that it may [endure] with yow togyther with age and years, and no doubt that will cause you to grow unto honestie and worshippe (as yow see in me today), and also bring yow to the honor and felicitie of the kingdom....

The St Paul's Sermon

This sermon predates the Gloucester sermon, having been preached towards the end of the fifteenth century, between 1489 and 1496. It was written for the boy by John Alcock, Bishop of Ely.

The quotation used to introduce this sermon is from the beginning of Psalm 112: *Laudate, Pueri, Dominum [Praise the Lord, you children/servants]*. While John Stubs's sermon relied very much on rhetorical effect, this sermon has a far more distinct philosophical basis.

It is also carefully crafted, linking the arguments together in a firm framework. Firstly, the boy examines man and his ability to direct his own path; then he argues the necessity of God's grace. As he identifies the three stages of life and their characteristics he inserts a set of prayers, pausing to add some humour at his own expense and that of his old schoolmasters. There then follows an examination of God's law in the Old Testament compared with that in the New Testament. The threefold division in man's life is paralleled with the threefold division of each month before he makes his final exhortation.

Initially, the boy explains that things which have a perfect understanding are able to dispose themselves to achieve their true goal because they possess real knowledge; but those things which lack understanding have no knowledge of themselves and so can only be brought to their natural goals with the assistance of another. Therefore animals, men especially, are able to direct themselves towards this end, but an arrow cannot reach a target unless it be shot.

> All those thynges that have the habyte of parfyght cognycyon may move themselves and conveye themselves to theyre end, as a beest havynge sensible knowledge, and man more parfyghter, both sensyble and intellygyble, may themself whether they wyll, and so coneveye al theyr accyons and dedes to theyr naturall ende; …those thynges that lacke cognycyon, have no mocyon of themself, nother be directed to theyr ende without the helpe of an other. As an arrow of himself can not be movyd ne directed unto the prycke without the redy conveyaunce of hym that shoteth…

Having established that all people have the ability to achieve their goals, he sets out what the true goal of mankind is; and that is to come close to God.

> To this ende man, havynge the use of reason and parfyte knowlege, is directed by his free wyll as by a pryncypall in himself to move hym to God.

Nevertheless, to reach God, reason and knowledge are insufficient in themselves, for faith is also a requirement.

> And also by faith as a pryncypall above naturall knowlege, without the whiche it is impossible to plese God and attayne to the ende of grace in this present lyf and glory in heven.

It follows, then, that children who lack the reason and understanding of adults are more in need of God's grace. This is what lies behind their first lessons in school where they learn to pray for Christ's assistance.

> In token herof childerne newely sette to scole… have a recourse to God's dyreccyon, fyrste lernyge this (Cristis Crosse be my spede).

Since there is firm philosophical grounding to this sermon, it follows the medieval pattern of philosophical discourse by quoting authorities, including classical philosophers to add weight to the arguments. Referring to Pythagoras and Saint Isidorus, the boy explains how the letter *y* symbolises the ages of childhood and adolescence. The straight line of the letter can be said to represent infancy where the child is inclined neither to virtue nor to vice. But after childhood, the second stroke of the letter needs to be considered. This oblique line indicates a propensity towards vice. The writer probably regards adolescence as beginning at a much earlier age than we do, i.e. straight after infancy. It is this age that will prove to be the making or the breaking of the child.

> *...for this letter y is made of two lynes; one is a right line, the other is half ryght and half crokyd. And soo verily the Infant age of a childe is ryght neyther disposed to vertue neyther to vyce... But the seconde age is called Adolescencia, and hath two lynes, a ryght and a crokyd, sygnefyenge the dysposycion that he hath thenne to vyce and thenne to virtue. In the whiche age is the brekynge of every chylde to goodness or to lewdness.*

This age, the writer claims, is the hardest to understand; in fact even Solomon wittily affirmed that he was mystified by it. Every generation, it seems, has trouble understanding its children.

> *"Thre thynges (sayth Salomon) bene harde to me to knowe, and the fourth utterly I knowe not. The flighte of the egle in the ayer; The way of the serpent on the erthe; The sayllyng of a shyppe in the see; But the fourth and moost hardest is to understande the waye of a man in his growynge age."*

Though children lack adult understanding, we can rejoice that those such as the Holy Innocents can be saved by God's grace.

> *Tho children thenne the whiche lacke dyscrecyon, use of reason, and parfyght cognycyon, and yet attayne to the ende that is prepared for mannes blysse, as thyse blessyd Innocentes whoos solempnyte we halowe this daye...*

As in the Gloucester sermon, the foundation having been established, the boy then exhorts his audience to pray for all of the Church, but most especially for himself that he may never more be troubled by the *"waking rod"* of the prophet Jeremias, a reference to the punishment he has received at school. He ruefully recounts the effects of his past punishments and, spotting his old schoolmaster, he claims still to be frightened of him, despite his currently exalted position. This boy, like Richard Stubs, was obviously thought by the writer to be capable of using some humour to good effect.

> *whan the good Lorde askyd of Jeremye, Quid tu vides, Jeremia? [What do you see, Jeremias?] he answered and sayd Virgam vigilantem ego video, "A waken rodde I see," sayd Jeremye. Truely thys waken rodde oftentymes hath troubled me in my childehood, that lumbi mei impleti sunt illusionibus, et non est sanitas in carne meo; afflictus sum et humiliatus sum nimis [My loins are chastised by my visions, and there is no health in me; I am greatly afflicted and humiliated] and therefor, though I be now in hye dygnyte, yet whan I see other here my mayster that was thenne, operuit confusio faciem meam, a voce contremuerunt labia mea [my face was covered in confusion; at his voice my lips trembled]*

The humour now takes on a harsher aspect as the boy hopes for his master (whom he says with bitter sarcasm that he loves so well) the same that Nero wished for his schoolmaster, Seneca – that he would do away with himself. Warming to his theme, he hopes that all his masters might be promoted to the court of the King's Bench and then, so that the end of their lives might be just as blessed, that they find their way to the *Via Tiburtina*; which is as much as to say that he would like to see them tried, convicted and hanged at Tyburn. No meek, sycophantic milksop this boy – no dressed up, cute moppet.

> *As Nero the Emperour wold to his mayster Seneca, the same wysshe I wold to my master I love soo well. And for theyr true dylygence that all my masters the whiche taughte me ony connynge in my youth gave to me, I wolde they were promytted to be perpetual felowes and collegeners of that famous college of the Kynges foundacyon in Southwerke that men calle the Kynges Benche... And for by cause*

charyte is parfyght yf it be extended as well to the ende of lyf as it is the lyf itself, I wolde they sholde ende ther lyf in that holy way... callyd in Latyn Via Tiburtina: in Englysshe asmoche to saye as the highe waye to Tyburne.

He next asks for the people to pray that all those who become bishops may achieve that station as he himself has done, without any false dealing. The cleverly implied criticism, perhaps even of his own bishop, surely suggests some courage on the part of the boy, or at least on the part of the writer.

...ye shall praye specyally for all prelates that cometh to theyr dygnytee as I dyde; for, thanked be God wythout conspyracy, lordshyp or symony [16]

After asking for prayers for the Church, he then asks for prayers for the temporal rulers of the kingdom and of the city of London.

Our soverayne lorde the Kyng. Our soverayne lady the Quene, My lorde the Prynce, My lady the Kynges Moder, My lorde her Husbonde, with all the Lordes of the Realme; the welfare of this Cyte, for my ryght worshypful broder and lover the Mayer, with all the Aldermen and Shyrefs.

Then he prays for *"all the soules lyenge in the paynes of Purgatory."*

With the exhortations to prayer completed, the boy begins the main section of his sermon by repeating the quotation from the psalm *Laudate, Pueri, Dominum.* He explains in terms that we have encountered before, that children's innocence should be imitated because they are *"pure in clennesse from sinne and malice"*. However, that is not to say that children's undeveloped *"wyttes"* should be copied. The psalmist exhorts children to praise the Lord but the boy thinks it befitting that men in all periods of life should offer praise as innocent children.

...I saye Laudate, pueri, Dominum; Laudate, pueri, Dominum in infantia; laudate Dominum in adolescentia; laudate Dominum in perseverante etate humana.

The three ages: infancy, adolescence and manhood, can be regarded as the *Lawe of Kynde, the Lawe Wryten, and the Lawe of Grace*. Infants are subject to the Law of Kind (Nature) and they cannot be held responsible for any faults. However they do need guidance lest they fall into water or fire. Mankind in its infancy, lacking the law of God, ran to destruction, as at the time of Noah's Flood, or the obliteration of Sodom and Gomorrah. The boy notes the lack of suitable masters and nurses to guide society and worries that they may all be corrected by water and fire.

> *A chylde fyrste when he is in his infant age… there is no defaute*
> *layde unto hym, but utterly he is lefte unto the lawe of kynde.*
> *Morally the state of man inmedyatly after synne was verily the state*
> *of childenhode and infans havinge no nouryce… Correccyon was*
> *there none, but utter destruccyon, as Noes floode, destroyenge all*
> *infants of mankyde save viij persones (Genesis vij) The destruccyon of*
> *Sodome and of Gomor with other cytees (Genesis xix). And lyke wyse*
> *as a childe, havynge noo nouryce nor guyder deputed to hym, may as*
> *well renne in to the fyre or water as to go beside, soo verily in the*
> *fyrste age of man… And verily, Maysters, yf we clerely consydre our*
> *lyf and state that we stande in now in thyse dayes, I fere me we shall*
> *fynde ourself soo ferre guyded by our sensuall nature, that we shall*
> *need to be purefyed to our streyte correccyon wyth a streyte afflyccyon,*
> *as the water or the fyre.*

The lack of spiritual and temporal guidance is at the root of the problem. In the Church is to be found bad behaviour and worldly talk, while in society at large there is massive distortion of morality, for sins are no longer accounted as such, being reckoned by other acceptable names. The result of this is that the once prosperous kingdom now exists in misery; dissimulation rules; Anger, Murder and Falsehood have replaced Peace, Love and Charity; and Truth has fallen. Some thought that Truth had fallen in Lombard Street (the street of bankers) or Bucklersbury (known for its gold and silver exchanges) but it was discovered that it has fallen in every street, and all for the want of masters and guides. Even in that period it was convenient to hold bankers responsible for the ills of society.

> *…somtyme our reame was prosperous, now it is in mysery; somtyme*
> *Ryghtwysnesse was the cheyf ruler, now Falshede is quarter-master;*

*sometime was inhabytaunt Peas, Love and Charyte, now Wrathe
and Manslaughter and false Dyssymulacyon; somtyme Trouth was
mayster of our marchauntes, (nunc vero usura et dolus). And
somtyme Trouth stode upright, now he is fallen. Good men have
inserchyd the street where he felle; some sayde he fell in Lombarde
Strete, some sayde in Buklarsbury. And whan it was utterly knowe
he was fallen in every street (Veritas corruit in plateis), the cause is
none other but we lacke our maysters and guyders that sholde streytly
attende in this Infant age of condycyon that we bene in.*

The boy continues his analogy by describing the method by which children are taught
after leaving infancy. Every fault is corrected, sometimes by wringing the ears,
sometimes with a ferule on the hand, and sometimes by a beating with a rod. In like
manner, mankind out of its infancy was corrected by the "schoolmaster" Moses, who
taught the basic principles of the law: what was owing to God and what to
neighbours. God required oblations, sacrifices and tithes; neighbours were owed alms
and forgiveness. But the commandments at that time were strict and demanded an
ear for an ear and a tooth for a tooth without mercy. Even something as comparatively
minor as gathering sticks on the Sabbath was to be punished by stoning to death.
Mercy, however, beseeched God to send a new master who would be more gentle.

*Somtyme he wryngeth hym by the eeres. Sometyme he geveth hym a
stripe on the honde wyth the ferell. Some tyme beteth hym sharpely
with the rodde... As mankynde grewe in age almighty God provided
to man an enfourmer that was called Moyses, the whiche sholde
teche man his pryncypalles and small and rude doctrynes... Also he
taught hym how he sholde gyve to God his partes: the whyche were
sacrefyces, oblacyons and tythes... To our neyghbour mercyfully geve
oure almesse, and pyteously forgyve offences and dettes to theym that
bene nedy and maye not paye... In Moyses tyme streyte
commaundememtes were gyven to Man, streyte punysshmentes and
sharpe correccyons; they were taken by the eere streytly, whan it
commaunded in the Lawe aurem pro aure, dentem pro dente,
without ony mercy. He that gadred styckes on Sabot daye was stoned
unto the dethe... mercy cryed to almighty God to sende mankinde a
newe mayster that sholde entreate hym and teche more curtously*

With the coming of Christ, God made flesh, to tender a new law with love and kindness, so the third age, the mature years, of mankind began. Under this new law, where we are schooled in merciful kindness and gentleness, although yet we may fail, provided that we always strive to mend our ways, Christ will be content with us. Being now of man's estate, it behoves us to correct ourselves in the school of mercy under pain of feeling the force of the righteous sword of correction. We must be careful in all ages of life to praise God with the pure children and to amend our lives with penance and good deeds so that we may be open to the invitation *"Praise the Lord, you children".*

> *...and it lyked him to come downe hymself and toke on hym pure mortallyte, gave us a newe law, wolde suffer none but hymselfe to be oure mayster; where with all love and benygnyte, without sharpnesse, he taught us noo rude nother grose erthly doctrynes, as they were taughte in the olde lawe... And as longe as we bene in the scole of mercyfull benygnytee and gentylnesse, though we doo fawtes, purposynge to amende, soo longe he abydeth us pacyently, holdyinge hymself content. For by cause we bene now in mannes state and parfyght age with oure owne correccyon.... And yf we dyfferre and wyll not correcte our selfe here in the scole of mercy, full grevously and moost sharply shall we abyde the swerde of correccyon of his ryghtwysnesse, as dayly by experyence we maye fele. Therefor, in the thre ages of oure lyf lette us besye ourselfe to prayse God wyth pure childerne, amendynge our lyfe by dedes of penaunce and virtuouse dedes usynge, exhortynge you with wordes of my tyme [theme] – Laudate, pueri, Dominum.*

To develop this concept of three stages the boy finds a parallel in the calendar and its division of each month into the *Kalendas, Nonas,* and *Ydus* following the custom of the ancient Romans. Each of the three divisions represents one of the ages of man. Although this section will in all likelihood seem to us a rather lengthy and laboured argument, the medieval mind delighted in finding such parallels and exploring their depths, squeezing every possible significance from them.

The conclusion of the sermon focuses on reminding the audience that a man's life can be divided into two parts: that of vice and that of virtue. But if a life is so divided, like a divided coat, it cannot be made whole again. It is hard, the boy insists, quoting St Jerome, for a man to have all his joy in this world and also in heaven. Thus it is a wise man who keeps his soul, like his coat, whole in virtue. He hopes that all may follow the innocent path of the Holy Innocents and, if sinning, will seek the grace to amend. The boy ends with the earnest desire that Christ would grant to all people the crowns of the Innocents.

> *And whyle it is so that man lyveth here in two lyves, one lyvynge after the pleasur of the worlde, the tother lyvynge here in vertue by grace to come to blysse, tho that woll geve one partye of theyr lyfe to vyces and another to vertue, and specially in theyr age, thyse maner of men dyvyde theyr cote, and they, nother all the tayllers in the worlde, shall never make it hole ayen: for as saynt Jerome sayth in a pystle, Difficile, ymmo impossibile est, ut quis in praesenti et in futuro fruatur gaudiis, ut hic ventrem et ibi mentem, et de deliciis transiat – "It is harde, ye it is impossyble, that a man may have alle joye in this worlde and also in heven – here to fylle his body and there to fylle his mynde;" for truly the delytes of this worlde and the joyes of heven can never be togyder in one cote of thy soule... And that the ende may be conformable to his pryncyple without dyvysion, followynge the wayes of Innocency with thyse holy Innocents in whose commendacions syngeth our moder holy chirche, Novit Dominus viam Innocentum qui non steterunt in viis peccatorum [The Lord knows the way of the Innocents who did not stand in the ways of sin]. And yf we be in synne to repare ourselfe to the state of grace without the wyll to falle again. And in recognysaunce of this gracyous benefyte of remyssyon we may lovingly prayse God as I exhortyd you before, sayeng, Laudate, pueri, Dominum, graunt us all, Cryste Jhesus Splendor Patris, corona Innocencium.*

Erasmus's sermon

There is some debate about the third sermon, written by Erasmus in the time of Dean Colet, over whether it was written for the ceremonies of the Boy Bishop, or merely just for preaching in St Paul's School. However, the external evidence suggests that it was indeed a Boy Bishop sermon, for in his statutes for the school Colet laid down that:

> *All these children shall every Childremas daye come to Paull's Churche and here the Childe Bishoppes sermon, and after be at highe masses, so eache of them offer a i d. to the Childe Bishopp, and with the Maisters and Surveyours of the Scoole. In generall processions, when they be warnyde, theye shall go tweyne and twenye to gather soberly, and not singe oute, but saye devoutly tweyne and tweyne vii salmes with latanye* [17]

Yet this is a sermon very different in content from the other two. Even given that the boys were attending the ancient Boy Bishop ceremonies, how the spirit of the reformers infects this sermon. Gone is the life, the vigour, the colour, the daring, the wit and the edge and in their place a plodding condescension. One is left to conclude that Erasmus, for all his great learning, hardly understood the character of boys. It is difficult to believe that after listening to this hugely lengthy sermon the boys would have been moved to alter their ways at all. What seems to add to the monotony of the day is that after having been corralled to the cathedral in pairs saying psalms (without even the chance of singing) and having been forced to sit through the tedium of the preaching, there is no evidence to suggest that the schoolboys were in any way allowed to enjoy the festivities traditionally associated with the feast.

The rather priggish tone of the sermon is established at the start. This boy admits his lack of eloquence, as did Richard Stubs, but then sententiously makes a virtue out of this failing.

> *I, a chylde, goynge aboute to speake before children of the ineffable chylde Jesus, wyll not wyshe the eloquence of Tullie* [18]*, which myghte stryke the eares with shorte and vayne pleasure. For how much Chrystes wisdom is in dystaunce from the wisdom of the worlde (the dystaunce is unmeasurable), so much ought the christen eloquence dyfferre from the eloquence of the worlde.*

It is possible, even from these few words to detect the influence of the reformers, not only in that the focus has moved from the Holy Innocents to the person of Christ himself, but there is also that fear of "pleasure". The sheer length of this sermon precludes any detailed analysis but its main lines of thought can be summarised.

The boy hopes that he may be the means by which his audience may receive heavenly grace.

> *...that he, from whose body flodes of lyuyshe [living] water do renne, wyll vouche salue [vouchsafe] by the instrument of my voice, as it were by the pipe of a conduyt, to flowe into the myndes of all you, with the plenteous moisture of hevenly grace to water them.*

Once more, there can be detected the thrust of the reformist agenda: words are to be the means of communicating God's grace.

He suggests that in the war with evil, Christ will be their military captain. He argues that soldiers and schoolboys will be encouraged to fight manfully if: they come to admire their captain; they love him; and there is a reward. The structure of the whole sermon is structured on these three points but it lacks the customary prayers, seen in the other two sermons. The boy argues in great detail why Christ is worthy of admiration. The flavour of the sermon can be gauged from the following extract which is one of the more striking parts.

> *Now, syr, what can be ymagyned more ample than he, whiche beynge infounded [poured] through all, yet restreyned in no place, abydeth in hymselfe uncompassable and unmeasurable? What is more ryche than he, which is the very chyef and principall goodness; from whome all good thynges do issue, and yet he is not therby dyminyshed? What is more renoumed that he, whiche is the renoume of his fathers glorie, and whiche onely "lygthtneth every man commynge into this worlde?"* [19] *What is more mighty than he, to whome the father almighty "hath gyven all power in heven and in earthe?"* [20] *What is of more force than he, whyche with a symple becke made all; at whose commaundement the see falleth, the shapes [appearances] of things be turned, the diseases flee, the armed fall downe, the devils are driven away, the elements obey, the rocks of stone are cutte in sonder, the dead wax a lyve agayne, the sinners be converted, finally all thynges be made new?*

The piling up of details in lengthy lists and use of rhetorical questions are common features of this sermon, but being extended in this way it must have seemed interminable to those boys penned in and forced to listen.

The second part of the sermon lists the reasons why Christ should be loved. In the small extract that follows, the listing technique is again employed, but with a sophisticated structure. There are lists within the list and a patterning of statements with purpose clauses, all with a certain raw power in the choice of vocabulary.

> *Thou tokest upon the [thee] our humanitie, to call us to the felowshyp of thy divinitye. Thou dydest put upon the this our slyme, to the entent thou myghtest cladde [clothe] us with the glorie of immortaltie. Beynge covered in our shape, thou woldest lyve many yeres with us in this wretched worlde, that thou myght bryng us yea [indeed] thus in to the love of the. Naked, thou crepst up into this light, nay nyght rather. With us, nay, for us, thou didst crye lyke a babe; thou dydst hunger, thurst, suffer heate, cold, labour, wetynes, neade, watchynge, fastynge; and to so many evils of ours thou woldeste be thrall; to the entente thou shuldest bryng us exempted from all evils into the communion of the; that is to say of the hyghe joy.*

The reward for following Christ as captain is, of course, eternal life.

> *...who in this transitorie lyf wolde not judge it lyte and swete, whereby he getteth that hevenly lyfe, and which shal never forsake him: to raygne eternally with Christ; to behold continually that high joy and goodness; to be conuersant in the companye of aungels; to be farre from all feare of evils?*

The conclusion to the sermon contains the sort of exhortation to be found in the other two sermons.

> *Wherefor let us lyve in him a pure and angelycal lyfe...*

Unlikely to have been especially receptive to the brilliant but seemingly interminable construction of the sermon,[21] how the boys must have wriggled in their seats, longing for release.

Other sermons

The sermons probably formed an important part of the ceremonies in most places where there was a suitable adult with the time and ability to write one. Thus there was a sermon preached at Bristol where the Mayor, Sheriff and others were to *"walk to St Nicholas' Church, there to heare theire even-song, and on the morrow to hear their mass and offer, and hear the boy-bishop's sermon, and have his blessing."* [22] In Spain it seems that it was the custom for the Boy Bishop preaching the sermon to pretend that he was one of the Innocents who had escaped death at the hands of Herod's soldiers. [23]

Scripts from the careful pen of an educated adult these sermons may be, yet it took a boy with some confidence and ability to deliver them successfully. He must have acquired at least some of the abilities of the orator, or showman, for surely a mere reading of the words, especially of the first two sermons, would have been absurd and unacceptable. The demands made by preaching illustrate in a different way how the boy would have needed to have developed adult skills and an early sense of responsibility. In many ways medieval boys grew up quickly.

Control, Suppression and Decline

Given the nature of the Boy Bishop ceremonies, it is only to be expected that attempts were frequently made to curb excesses or to suppress them completely. The rigorist and the lenient forever stand toe to toe, fists clenched and draw up their battle lines. The conflict between the dogmatist and the latitudinarian, the fundamentalist and the liberal is ageless. The Boy Bishop ceremonies had from early times come under the harsh, judgemental gaze of those who could see only occasions for mischief and sin. Others, who could tolerate the essentially harmless, rougher edges of humanity, defended and clung onto what they saw as an ancient, festive custom which helped to teach the Christian message to young and old alike.

As far as concerns the Boy Bishop ceremonies, sometimes specific abuses occasioned reform or suppression; at other times high-held principles were applied to control or abolish them. Perhaps in most places the ceremonies just faded away in a changing world.

Ironically it was the popularity of the ceremonies that occasionally directed the cold attention of those in authority. In Salisbury they had proved such an attraction that, when enthusiastic crowds packed the cathedral to witness the Boy Bishop's procession, the press of people had unfortunately proved so great that serious injuries and damage had resulted. As a consequence in 1319 Bishop Roger de Mortival enacted statutes to control the problem.[1] Under pain of excommunication people were forbidden from rashly contravening the liberties, and peace and quiet of the Church; in addition it was forbidden to check or impede in any way the boys' procession. All were enjoined to take part in the procession, but out of devotion to behave themselves in an adult manner for the glory of God, just as they were used to do for other processions. To prevent problems which had arisen from his visitations, the Boy Bishop was forbidden from enjoying any visitations either within or outside the cathedral precincts. Instead he was limited to conversing with his companions in the common house, unless he was invited by a canon to be entertained at his table. However, even these tight restrictions did not prevent the murder in 1448 and further restrictions followed, as described in Chapter 1.

It was not always the case that ceremonies of the Boy Bishop created controversy, for they wore the mantle of respectability when compared with the Feast of Fools, which was far more frequently the object of censure. Something of this can be gleaned from a letter published in France.[2] The writer who was no supporter of this type of ceremony in general has nothing but praise for what he witnessed. He considers that what had formerly been a scandal had become something to edify the faithful. At St Omer he was delighted with the quality of the boys' singing during the different parts of the Mass, so much so that he recounts being *"enchanted, touched"* by their modesty and innocence, recognising a certain seriousness married with the natural graces of childhood. The procession, too, was a model of dignity. This all provided a very good presentation of the Catholic religion. It went to show that when the ceremonies were performed well, even those disposed to oppose them could be converted. However, at St Peter's in Lille the differences from the Feast of Fools were not enough to save the Boy Bishop ceremonies. Although no one thought that any abuses had occurred during these ceremonies, it was decided to abolish them along with the Feast of Fools, because it did not seem expedient to allow the choristers special privileges.[3] Yet, since it was acknowledged that the youngsters' ceremonies posed little threat to the good order of the church, the Boy Bishop was revived almost immediately and continued for more than half a century after the more chaotic celebrations of his elders had disappeared for ever. Even when the Boy Bishop was finally abolished at St Peter's, a less controversial title of *abbé de choraux* was granted and the chapter continued to provide some entertainment for the choirboys as a memorial to the famous feast.

In Laon in 1521, rules were made to regulate the Boy Bishop's ceremonies, but these were never observed,[4] although the festivities there did give sufficient reason for suppression.[5] After Mass the choristers and the pupils of the schools run by the clergy presented a mystery play in the centre of the nave. Once the show was over, the boys and clergy rushed through the city in a procession with farses, grimacing and relating dirty stories. Each canon having a cassock trailing behind him tried to step on the cassock of the one in front, to the laughter and amusement of the whole city. The day ended with a dinner. These indecent shows with their ribaldry caused so much scandal to the cathedral that Fleury believed them to have been abolished by the end of the fifteenth century. However, the Boy Bishop ceremonies in many places were possessed of a remarkable resilience and they continued in Laon until at least the end of the sixteenth century.[6]

It was a similar story in Bayeux. The chapter ordered the suppression of the ceremonies in 1482, the result, as they saw it, of certain abuses.[7] Yet the accounts of the Abbey of the Holy Trinity show that they must have continued at least until 1546, for in that year the Abbey made a donation to the Bayeux Boy Bishop of five sous.[8]

In Sens the war with the English, concluded in 1420, had long term consequences for the finances of the cathedral and the chapter found itself unable to afford the type of expenditure it had enjoyed in the past.[9] The ceremonies of the Boy Bishop suffered severe reductions in the chapter's financial support. As the financial support faded, so did the clergy's ability to control the ceremonies, with the result that, because the boys and young clerics no longer felt such a strong obligation to the chapter, the chants were turned into confusion, the pious dramatic representations into grotesque masquerades and ceremonies which had supported the faith were turned against it. Added to this, the disorder resulting from the war had proved to be an additional temptation to the boys and young clerics to indulge in questionable behaviour. The seriousness of the situation, not only in France but also in neighbouring lands, prompted the famous decree from the Council of Basel. This decree entitled *De spectaculis in ecclesia non faciendis [Concerning spectacles not to be performed in church]* covered the Feast of Fools, the Boy Bishop and other like feasts. It condemned the practice of dressing certain persons with mitre and staff who would then bless men after the manner of bishops, and the dances and festivities that followed. However, the Feast of Fools was to fare worse yet, for in a letter sent to all the bishops and chapters in France the Faculty of Theology in Paris endeavoured to rally support for the complete suppression of that feast. Nevertheless, the chapter of Sens decided that after so many years of tolerating and encouraging the feast it would be impracticable suddenly to abolish it. The feasts continued to be celebrated at Sens as the power of custom prevailed over continued efforts to abolish them, and they did prove to be most resilient indeed. Next both the Feast of Fools and the Boy Bishop were condemned by a provincial council in 1528 but still they flourished until at least 1547. The memory of the Boy Bishop lingered somewhat longer, for in the nineteenth century the choir boys used to imitate bishops on Holy Innocents' Day, calling their Archbishop *"âne"* which related back to the ass from the Feast of Fools.[10]

Louis Petit de Julleville recorded that about 1550 the Feast of the Innocents was still celebrated in many cities as it had been since the twelfth century.[11] The willingness to forget inconvenient regulations had a long history in France. As far back as 1260 the Council of Cognac (*Copriniacense*) had forbidden dancing in the church on Holy Innocents' Day as well as disturbances and disputes, under the threat of excommunication.[12] The election of the bishop was also forbidden. Obviously these restrictions scarcely had any effect, as Du Cange noted. And neither the Synod of Carnot which had tried to prevent foolish behaviour and the apparel of fools in church, nor the Synod of Aix in 1585 which forbade all mockery and games associated with Holy Innocents' Day, nor the Synod of Toulouse in 1590 forbidding plays and spectacles in churches and graveyards, seem to have be aimed at suppressing the Boy Bishop.[13]

Péronne, where the last Boy Bishop, Desjardin, had been elected as late as 1638, had experienced some troubles with the ceremonies in the past.[14] The chapter had been in the custom of providing wine and food for the festivities, but it seems that some of the clergy had scandalised the townsfolk by taking supper at the *Hôtel-Dieu*. In February 1604 the chapter condemned this behaviour, imposed a fine and imprisoned one canon for eight days, since it was a repeat offence. At Noyon the Dean, Jacques Le Vasseur (who had been a Rector of the University of Paris), thoroughly disapproved of his colleagues' attempts to reform the ceremonies. He drew attention to their tradition of over 400 years in the cathedral and declared with some irritation, *"O wretched age!"*, thinking that the reformers were no more than beasts hiding behind the robes and beards of philosophy.[15] The ceremonies were not finally abolished until 1721.[16] Certainly by the mid-nineteenth century the only traces in Picardy of the once magnificent ceremonies were that in some places the choristers could sing the Office or the *Hi sunt (These are they)*, or perhaps beat time.

Although the Synod of the Diocese of Chartres had cause to try to ensure decent behaviour in 1525 by demanding that *"on the feast of St Nicholas, St Catherine, Innocents' or any other day, under the colour of recreation, no school-boys, clerks, or priests shall do anything foolish and laughable in church"*,[17] it appears that the Boy Bishop might have survived until at least 1724.[18]

In Tournai, the customs of the Feast of Fools seem to have displaced the ceremonies of the Boy Bishop, for the Synod wrote condemning the practice of allowing comically dressed characters to appear in church on Holy Innocents' Day and St Nicholas's Day, because they were a scandal, corrupting instead of edifiying.[19]

Things took a slightly different course in the schools in the south and west of Germany. As early as 1274 a Salzburg synod banned adults from any participation in the ceremony of the Boy Bishop. Clearly, as in other places, they had been the cause of the problems. Only boys of sixteen years and younger were to be permitted to participate and the boys' role in the liturgy was entirely abolished. Yet, not all the misbehaviour could be blamed on the adults, for in 1249 the pupils of Regensburg, accompanied by other inhabitants from the villages of Mummem and Larven, marched against the neighbouring abbey of Prüfling with the Boy Bishop at their head.[20] On being refused admittance by the abbot, they forced the gates, ill-treated the domestics and drove the cattle out of the cattle sheds. The guilty initially seemed to have escaped punishment, but the matter did not end there. The abbot, having failed to receive justice, appealed to the Holy See. Pope Innocent IV issued a command to the Bishop of Regensburg that in future he was to ensure that pupils did not harass the abbey in any way. It is, perhaps, a mistake to attribute this violence solely to the Boy Bishop ceremonies, for the account seems to contain sufficient evidence to suggest that the villagers and others harboured a grudge against the abbey.

At Eichstädt the boys had only themselves to blame when the ceremonies were abolished by Bishop Reimboto in 1282. In this part of Germany the boys were especially privileged for the ceremonies began on 6th December and continued for the three weeks until 28th December, being paid for by the *scholares canonici* who had completed their studies and who had achieved the status of independence. In celebration of their new status they were expected to meet the expenses of the school festival, but in a spirit of competition they aimed each year to outdo the previous years in the magnificence of the festivities provided. In this way fortunes were spent and the holy festival of Christmas was desecrated by extravagance and indulgence. What was worse, bloody fights sometimes broke out. The penalties for breaking the bishop's ban indicated how seriously he took the abuses, for they comprised heavy fines and excommunication.

Fights had also broken out in Worms resulting in citizens making complaints to the bishop, who, because of the grave nature of the offences, allowed the pupils to hold their processions only on St Nicholas's Day, the Eve of St Lucy, Christmas Day and the three days following. They were most strictly forbidden from marching along the streets and from singing after the festivities had ended. From the end of the thirteenth century, the choristers here found their privileges increasingly denied during Christmas-tide. The Boy Bishop was suppressed in Lubeck in 1336, but he continued at Cologne until 1662, when he was abolished by Bishop Max Heinrich because his celebrations were deemed to be unfitting.

The ceremonies caused no great controversy at Mainz and they never came under official censure.[21] It was explained the prohibitions of the Council of Basel did not affect the celebrations because these were aimed at suppressing the excesses of the Feast of Fools which had never become prominent at Mainz. Some of the celebrations survived until at least 1779.[22]

The Boy Bishop's time was also coming to an end in Spain. There had been attempts to suppress the excesses which seem to have been part of the Feast of Fools. The chapter of Vique in 1319 had abolished the use of a paraphrased vernacular epistle during Mass, while in 1473 the Council of Aranda had demanded an end of the introduction into the Liturgy of unseemly entertainments such as shows, secular songs, burlesques and masques which had begun to disturb people's devotions even during Mass.[23] The clergy were threatened with fines if they allowed these things to take place, or even condoned them. However, the Council did not want to forbid any performances that were an aid to devotion. Apparently, in Gerona the Boy Bishop had been accustomed to receiving people for Confirmation[24] along with other rather questionable behaviour. These unseemly activities were ended in 1541. Tarragon suppressed the ceremonies in 1566.[25] Between 1565 and 1566 the Council of Toledo ensured that, where the Boy Bishop ceremonies survived, the more rowdy elements were eliminated by prohibiting the objectionable theatrical elements and forbidding those in holy orders from wearing masks and disguises.

The situation at Seville was complicated. The archbishop, dean and chapter had already reformed the ceremonies in 1512, but it seems that by 1545 irreverence had slipped in again and that an attempt was made to abolish them as a consequence of *"the many contemptible things that happened"*.[26] But, as in France, popular opinion ran strongly against the reformers and the order was revoked on 20th November.[27] Nevertheless, changes were made. The Boy Bishop was forbidden to ride through the city as he was accustomed to do. In fact, he was ordered not to leave the cathedral and was directed to robe and disrobe in one of the chapels. However, the limited success was short-lived. Probably in an attempt to divorce the Boy Bishop from the Feast of Fools in 1562 the ceremonies were transferred to St Nicholas's Day, 6th December, but this simply foreshadowed their demise. The ceremonies were finally abolished in the cathedral in 1563.

However, the custom of celebrating the Boy Bishop was so deep-rooted that despite its abolition in the cathedral it continued in the school of Maese Rodrigo each year on St Nicholas's Day. As it turned out, these ceremonies provoked as much controversy as those in the Cathedral had done. In 1641 on the eve of St Nicholas's Day the Boy Bishop and his entourage went onto the streets causing a great disturbance at the school door, ordering laymen and priests to get out of their carriages in order to offer reverence to the Boy Bishop, D Esteban Dongo, by kissing his hand. The misbehaviour escalated for as the day drew on, not being satisfied with humiliating those passing by, the boys seized a carriage and went through the city committing all sorts of excesses, insulting both men and women and forcing judges and ministers to get out of their carriages when they came across them. In the evening they invaded the theatre and, amidst a great uproar interrupted the performance, which then had to be restarted. A brawl started as the boys tried to seize carriages from the horsemen who were waiting for their masters outside the theatre. This resulted in a number of injuries as the boys were armed with pistols, rifles, shields, swords and other weapons. This armoury perhaps explains how the boys managed to get away with so much earlier in the day. In the manner of boys, they had become carried away in the heat of the excitement in disregard of what the consequences were likely to be. Inevitably, there was a trial. Bartolomé Dongo, the Boy Bishop's father, a wealthy Genoese, was fined 500 or 1,000 ducats and the school was forbidden from ever celebrating the ceremonies again.

In Denmark the memory lingered until the nineteenth century when children used to elect a Yule Bishop dressed in a white shirt to whom a song was sung and nuts were given.[28]

The convents, too, were attracting the attention of those who sought to control the festivities. In 1275, by order of Archbishop Peckham, the parallel service to the Boy Bishop was forbidden in Godstow Abbey, where the girls were no longer allowed to conduct a liturgy[29] but obviously such innocent activities continued, for in 1526 a similar order was given to Carrow nunnery by the Bishop of Norwich.[30] The Archbishop of Rouen had tried to forbid similar activities in some of the convents in his diocese in the mid-thirteenth century, although, at least in Caen, the novices were still choosing an Abbess as late as 1423.[31] In the Abbaye aux Bois the Girl Abbesses held their place until at least 1773.[32]

Worries about inappropriate clothing form a common complaint. For example, the Order of Observant Franciscans forbade the use of secular clothing and the robes of the religious orders on St Nicholas's Day and Holy Innocents' Day.

It was quite probable that the Boy Bishop ceremonies in England were less likely to cause offence than elsewhere in Europe, since here they seem to have been more isolated from the influence of the Feast of Fools. In 1279, Archbishop

Peckham when creating the constitutions for religious houses had already attempted to limit the Boy Bishop celebrations to just two days: the eve and the day of Holy Innocents.[33] In York and St Paul's, London, as we have seen, the problems that arose were settled with carefully drafted statutes. There were two attempts at Wells in 1331 and 1338 to reform the behaviour of the priests, deacons and subdeacons in the cathedral, but there seems to have been no attempt to forbid them completely.[34] The same is true of Bishop Grandisson's injunctions to the clergy of Exeter Cathedral and the churches of Ottery St Mary, Crediton and Glasney.[35] But in both cases the criticisms seem to have been levelled more clearly at the sort of activities associated with the Feast of Fools. And so the ceremonies seem to have escaped the sporadic attempts at suppression that had been attempted elsewhere. This was all to change with Henry VIII, who in 1541 issued a proclamation on 22nd July.

> *Whereas heretofore dyvers and many superstitions and chyldysh observances have be[en] used, and yet to this day are observed and kept, in many and sundry parts of this realm, as upon Saint Nicholas, Saint Catherine, Saint Clement, the Holy Innocents and such like, children be strangelie decked and apparayled to counterfeit priestes, bishoppes, and women, and so be ledde with songes and daunces from house to house, blessing the people and gathering of money; and boyes do singe masse and preache in the pulpit, with suche other unfittinge and inconvenient usages, rather to the derysyon than any true glory of God, or honor of his sayntes: The Kynges Majestie therefore, myndinge nothinge so moche as to advance the true glory of God without vaine superstition, wylleth and commandeth that from henceforth all such superstitious observations be left and clerely extinguished throwout his realms and dominions, for asmuch as the same doth resemble rather the unlawfull superstition of gentilitie, than the pure and sincere religion of Christe.[36]*

Those under Henry's rule were inclined to take such proclamations seriously. There was no question of ignoring this command, as had been the case in some other countries where suppression had been unsuccessful, for the terror that Henry inspired was too powerful an agent of enforcement. Obviously Henry believed that he needed to suggest some reasons why such a popular feast was to be abolished, and it is interesting to see how he uses Protestant propaganda and persuasion. The negative noun *superstitions* and the description of the children as *"strangelie decked"* imply that such celebrations belong to "popish perversions" of the Christian message, while the use of the adjective *"chyldysh"* intimates that such practices should not find favour among those with an adult outlook. It must have been known that the boys never actually performed the specifically priestly actions of the Mass – although they did participate in it – yet Henry ambiguously claims that they *"do singe masse"* implying that they had usurped a purely sacerdotal function. There then follows the loaded phrase *"unfittinge and inconvenient usages"* which is no more than a broad statement of disapproval. Obviously, those who attended and supported the celebrations found them neither *"unfittinge"* nor *"inconvenient"*. The pompous and self-righteous claim of Henry that he wishes nothing so much as *"to advance the true glory of God without vaine superstition"* does little more than provide a hollow justification. Ironically, this proclamation adds additional weight to the evidence indicating that the abuses that occurred elsewhere were not tainting the English celebrations, for there is no mention of the excesses that had been condemned in France and Germany.

The restoration of Catholicism under Mary saw a revival of many ceremonies connected with holydays and included in these was the festival of St Nicholas. Thus the order came from Bishop Bonner.

> *The xiii day of November was commondyd by the bysshope of London to all clarkes in the dyoses of London for to have sant Necolas and to go a-brod, as mony as wold have ytt.*[37]

Strangely, on the eve of Saint Nicholas's Day, the previous order was revoked without any explanation being given.

> *The v day of December, the which was saint Nicholas' eve, at evensong time, came a commandment that seint Nicholas should not go abroad, nor about.*

Perhaps the stricter churchmen had won the day; perhaps it was thought that the ceremonies, especially in London, where the reformers were strong, would cause trouble, especially after the formal reconciliation with Rome on 30th November; or perhaps it was an indication of the new spirit of reforming Catholicism, evident in the reign of Mary, that was gaining ground in the Church and that would ultimately lead to the Council of Trent.

In any case, the ceremonies were too popular to be so easily cast aside and Machyn records that despite the countermand

> *...there went about these saint Nicholases in divers parishes, as st Andrew's, Holborn and st. Nicholas Olyffe in Bredstret.*

Not everybody's doors and hearts were opened to welcome the Boy Bishop's return. In his *Actes and Monuments* (Otherwise known as *Foxe's Book of Martyrs*) the Protestant polemicist, John Foxe recounts the following story.

> *In the late days of queen Mary, among other strange dealings of the papists with the faithful, this is not with the rest to be forgotten that a godly matron, named Gertrude Crockhay, the wife of master Robert Crockhay, dwelling then at St Katherine's by the Tower of London, abstained herself from the popish church. And she, being in her husband's house, it happened in anno 1556 that the foolish Popish Saint Nicholas went about the parish; which she understanding shut her doors against him, and would not suffer him to come within her house. Then Doctor Mallet, hearing thereof (and being master of the said Saint Katherine's) the next day came to her with twenty at his tail, thinking belike to fray her; and asked why she would not the night before let in St Nicholas, and receive his blessing, etc. To whom she answered thus: "Sir, I know no St Nicholas," said she, "that came hither." "Yes," quoth Mallet, "here was one that represented St Nicholas." "Indeed, sir," said she, "here was one that is my neighbour's child, but not St Nicholas: for St Nicholas is in heaven. I was afraid of them that came with him to have had my purse cut by them, for I have heard of men robbed by St Nicholas's clerks," etc. So Mallet, perceiving that nothing could be gotten at her hands went his way as he came, and she for that time so escaped.*[38]

The reservations of Foxe notwithstanding, the Boy Bishop continued to command the allegiance of people. Machyn noted that within two years of his restoration the popularity of the Boy Bishop had grown.

> *The v day of December was Sant Necolas evyn, and Sant Necolas*
> *whentt a-brod in most part in London syngyng after the old fassyon,*
> *and was reseyvyd with a mony good pepulle in-to ther howses, and*
> *had myche good chere as ever they had, in mony plasses* [39]

There was also a poem, now lost, *The song of the Chyld-Bysshope, as it was songe before the Queenes Majestie*, containing 36 stanzas written for the Boy Bishop to recite (or perhaps sing) before Queen Mary at the Manor of St James in the Fields on Saint Nicholas's Day and Holy Innocents' Day. Warton explains that it was a *"fulsome panegyric on the Queen's devotion, in which she is compared to Judith, the Queen of Sheba and the Virgin Mary".*[40]

Another account with a chilling reference to that age of persecution comes from Ipswich where the Boy Bishop was led through the streets by the Master of the Grammar School *"for apples and belly-cheer, and whoso would not receive him he made heretics, and such as would also not give his faggot for Queen Mary's child [the Boy Bishop]".*[41]

The Boy Bishop reborn under Queen Mary had but a brief time to enjoy his resurgence, for he was again suppressed in England under the following reign of Queen Elizabeth. However, even those suppressions at the close of the Middle Ages did not provide the end of the story, for there appears to have been an unbroken tradition at the great Abbey of Montserrat, and the Propaganda College in Rome was said to have retained its Boy Bishop (reigning until Epiphany, 6th January) at least until the beginning of the twentieth century owing to a provision in the foundation documents; however, it is hard to ascertain how long he continued after this.[42]

In the twentieth century, as a consequence of the wide-ranging research, some clergymen were prompted to restore the Boy Bishop to their churches. How this was achieved and with what success is examined in Chapter 9 – *The Revival*.

Differences from the Feast of Fools

The Feast of Fools is itself an important area of study and it lies beyond the compass of this book to examine it in more than superficial detail. It is, however, instructive to see how this feast, sometimes so closely associated with the Boy Bishop, differed in important aspects, most obviously in the disorder which it often occasioned, but also in its liturgy and character.[1]

The Feast of Fools sometimes rejoices in the name, the Feast of Asses (or the Feast of the Ass), which perhaps imparts something of the flavour of this celebration. The 1445 letter from the Faculty of Theology in Paris gives a good idea of the type of behaviour to be encountered in and around a cathedral.[2]

> *The bad priests and clerks are seen during the holy offices with monstrous faces in the clothes of women, actors, or pimps. They are seen dancing in the choir, singing shameful songs, chewing black puddings over the edge of the altar while the priest celebrates Mass. They play at dice in the same place and use old shoe soles burning to act as incense. They run and jump without shame through the whole church and are then led through the town and its theatres in vulgar carts and wagons in disgraceful shows using indecent gestures and scurrilous and unseemly language for the amusement of those accompanying them and of the bystanders.*

The Faculty refused to accept the justification that such entertainments offered time-honoured means of amusement, seeing them more as the work of devils. Suspecting that mere persuasion and references to the authority of great saints and bishops might not be enough, dark threats followed: the Inquisition and the intervention of the State, with the penalties of imprisonment, loss of benefices, loss of reputation and exclusion from the holy altars. The righteous, and we have no reason to suppose the Faculty were anything but righteous men, often see evil in the entertainments of the less sophisticated and less well-educated. Coarse, irreverent and vulgar as the activities undoubtedly were, it required a certain self-righteous certainty and a supreme confidence in drawing that sometimes thin line between good and evil to actually demonise them

The closest we can come to understanding the Feast of Fools and its spirit is to consider it as part religious observance, part pantomime, part fancy-dress party, part carnival, with some elements of a protest march and satirical show.

The Feast of Fools is given a variety of names, the most common of which are *Festum Stultorum, Festum Fatuorum,* and *Festum Follorum.* In fact the term covers not just one feast but three or four. The deacons held their feast on St Stephen's Day (26th December), appropriately enough, since St Stephen was a deacon; the priests on St John the Evangelist's Day (27th December), with the justification that as an Apostle he exercised priestly functions; and the subdeacons on the Feast of the Circumcision of Christ (1st January). The choristers' feast, Holy Innocents' Day is sometimes included and sometimes not. The most prominent of the feasts tended to be that of the subdeacons, if only because their celebrations were more rowdy, sacrilegious and scandalous than the others. The subdeacons were one of the orders of the Church, yet until about the thirteenth century their order was not ranked among the major sacred orders of bishop, priest and deacon; it was regarded as a minor order, even though subdeacons assisted the priests at the altar alongside the deacons. It appears that since the priests, deacons and even the choristers had designated feasts, the subdeacons considered that they too ought to appropriate one for themselves, and settled on the rather inappropriate Feast of the Circumcision of Christ. The status of subdeacons in the church may go some way towards explaining their behaviour for they were frequently given the more menial tasks in cathedrals, often being despised by members of the higher clergy. What is also probably significant is that being in holy orders they were exempt from criminal prosecution in secular courts, any cases against them being tried in ecclesiastical courts.

The fact that the Feast of Fools sometimes took place on Holy Innocents' Day does not mean that the Boy Bishop took part in this feast: it seems to have been a separate celebration with some similar features, even if it appears to have been taken over at times by the Feast of Fools.

Much of what can be learnt about the Feast of Fools is contained within documents condemning it, seeking to reform it or demanding its suppression. There have been some attempts in more recent years to explain that the Feast of

Fools was not as bad as has often been suggested, that it was more usually under control than not and that it had a serious spiritual purpose.[3] Clearly the same teaching based on the *Magnificat* concerning the mighty being put down from their seats and the humble being raised up is emphasised in this feast just as it is in the Boy Bishop ceremonies. However, the regularity with which it attracted stern criticism and repeated complaints about continued abuses, indicate not only that the behaviour of the participants frequently ran to excess but that its customs were deeply ingrained and difficult to control. Moreover, if the Feast were to be banished entirely from the cathedral precincts there was the danger that once out of control of the chapter it might became even more profane.

The Feast of Fools never really achieved a very prominent position in England and, where it did gain a firm foothold as in Lincoln and Beverley, it did not seem to cause too much disruption and it was abolished with relatively little trouble; but in France it was a feast of some note and notoriety. It was already gaining its dubious reputation by the end of the twelfth century when the ceremony at Notre Dame was in need of reform.[4] Bishop Odo set about the task, creating a detailed set of instructions in his decree of 1198. The disrespectful behaviour on this feast was thought to be particularly inappropriate, given the calamities that were occurring across the world. The eve of the Circumcision was not to be marked by unusual ringing of the church bells. The use of poetry was controlled. There were to be no masques. It was forbidden to use extra candles in the cathedral or to allow the Lord of the Feast a procession either to or from the cathedral. The Lord was given the precentor's staff as a symbol of his position, and when it was handed over during the *Magnificat* it was prescribed that the *Deposuit* was to be sung no more than five times. From this instruction it is to be surmised that the staff would be handed to the subdeacon nominated the Lord of the Feast for the next year. This piece of ceremonial was in all likelihood the focus of raucous behaviour, for it can well be imagined that the out-going subdeacon "played to the gallery" by pretending to offer the staff first to one and then to another until the true candidate was selected, all to the accompaniment of shouts, importuning, mockery and laughter. The numerous repetitions of the *Deposuit* would have allowed this unworthy scene to have been played out at great length.

There is little remaining that shows the actual liturgy of the Feast of Fools. We can conjecture that the cathedral chapters would have deemed it foolish to commit too much to paper and besides much is a parody of liturgy rather than liturgy *per se*. However, the famous *Missel des Fous* at Sens does set out a detailed liturgy, but the whole set of offices for the feast contain only six extra elements that are found nowhere else in the liturgy of the cathedral, and these are not really objectionable.[5] The first, *Lux hodie* was sung at Vespers on the eve of the feast, outside the door of the cathedral and is a hymn of praise to the Light of the World who will banish misery and evil, and an invitation to the Feast of the Ass. The famous *Prose of the Ass* [6] was sung as the procession moved to the table where the names and duties were announced. Although at first sight this is a rather strange processional chant, it really just honours the ass who played his role in the Christmas story. He is honoured for his beauty and strength, for overcoming fallow deer, roebucks and camels, for bringing the gifts of gold, incense and myrrh and for eating the bearded barley and thistles. The ass is said to have crossed the Jordan into Bethlehem, but oddly there is no mention of the ass's part in saving the Christ Child by carrying him and the Blessed Virgin into Egypt. In some places an ass was brought into the cathedral but there is no mention of this at Sens. This prose is fairly harmless in itself, but mentions of the ass probably refer to earlier, less acceptable practices. The chorus *Hez, Sir Asne, Hez!* would give cause for some amusement with the onomatopoeic representation of the ass's braying. The third piece, sung towards the end of Matins, was accompanied by a procession. The text is unexceptionable being a hymn of praise to Christ who redeemed mankind, including the triumphant cry of *Natus est! Natus est! Natus est hodie Dominus… (He is born! He is born! The Lord is born today…)*. It seems likely that during the chant the procession approached the *bacularius* (the subdeacon to whom some authority was ceded) and he chanted the *Te Deum*. With the completion of this morning office, the participants went away to play games. The remaining three pieces were sung during Vespers of the feast itself. *Novus annus hodie* is a hymn of praise again celebrating Christ's redemption of mankind but also making reference to the place of singing and music-making in offering praise to God. *Kalendas ianuarias* includes the reference to the Roman feast of *Kalends* which some writers have seen as directly influencing the Feast of Fools. But this chant is no pagan song; it is entirely Christian in its references. *O crucifer, bone lucis sator*, of which the longer version was written by Prudentius, was to be recited before eating. Appropriately enough this too seems to have been sung before the company went to feast with a verse reminding all that the food and drink required Christ's blessing.

Since the feast at Sens had not experienced the same sort of criticism as elsewhere it might be concluded that the festivities here were more irreverent than sacrilegious, vicious or destructive, perhaps the successful result of the reforms initiated by Bishop Odo in Paris in 1198 and by Pierre de Corbeil (a signatory to Odo's decree, while he was canon of Notre Dame), who in all probability devised the first proper liturgy for the Feast of Fools at Sens.

The feast at Beauvais did include the ass in the liturgy.[7] After Lauds, the canons left the church and found an ass at the door of the cathedral. When the door was closed, the canons each took a bottle of wine and a glass, and the cantor intoned *Kalendas ianuarias*. They then battered on the door which was duly opened and the ass was escorted into the church accompanied by the singing of *The Prose of the Ass*. It seems likely that at Mass before the gospel, the censing was done using black-pudding and sausage. Tied up with the festivities of the Feast of Circumcision was a further feast on 14th January, the octave day of Epiphany, which celebrated the visit of the three wise men to the infant Christ. During this celebration, the Flight into Egypt was commemorated by the most beautiful girl in the city being placed on the ass with a representation of the Christ Child in her arms, and being taken to the neighbouring church of Saint Stephen with a procession made up of clergy and laity. At the church of Saint Stephen the ass was led up through the church and stationed at the altar. *The Prose of the Ass* was sung with a genuflection at the end, apparently to the ass, and the Mass finished with the priest dismissing the people and whinnying three times, to which the people responded with three whinnies *(In fine Missae sacerdos, versum ad populum, vice "Ita Missa est", ter hinhannabit: populus vero, vice "Deo, gratias", ter respondebit, "Hinham, hinham, hinham")*. In all likelihood the unreformed liturgies were more profane than these examples, as the letter from the Faculty of Theology of Paris indicates.

A complete exchange of garments often typified the Feast of Fools, the clergy dressing themselves in the everyday clothing of the people or even of fools, while the people donned the garb of priests and monks. This differed from the far more restrained Boy Bishop's ceremony where the swapping of robes was confined to the Boy Bishop himself, with perhaps some of those assisting him being permitted to wear silk copes. Apart from the obvious practical difficulties involved there seems to be no suggestion that the clergy ever clothed themselves in the boy choristers' robes.

All these liturgical alterations and parodies indicate how the manifestations of the spirit of the Feast of Fools can be differentiated from the Boy Bishop which remained a far more restrained and orthodox affair.

Some of the history of the Feast of Fools at Troyes will give sufficient indication of how difficult it was to control. In 1372 the chapter of St Peter's, one of the collegiate churches, made it a requirement that permission be granted before the feast could be celebrated. Even so, this proved inadequate to prevent the unruly behaviour that was so much a part of the celebration. The records show that damage was caused in the church in 1380 and in the following year. It was banned in 1439, but permitted once more in 1443 under certain conditions. The Lord of the Feast (in this case an Archbishop) was allowed to wear a bishop's rochet[8] but the festivities had to take place outside the church, and, in order to keep a tighter control over the behaviour of the participants, they were no longer permitted to hold their feast in an ale house but in a canon's house. Predictably, the canon proved unequal to the task, and he himself had to pay a fine for allowing unacceptable behaviour. Accordingly the bishop tried to prevent the feast from taking place the following year in any of the three churches in town. St Peter's agreed to abide by his decision, but at another of the churches, St Stephen's, the clergy refused to obey him, claiming that they came under the jurisdiction of the Archbishop of Sens. In an act of defiance, the feast of that year was more outrageous than usual. On the last Sunday in Advent the Archbishop was invested in public with a ceremony satirising the true consecration of a bishop. The Archbishop of Fools, having presided at the offices on the eve of the Circumcision and on the day itself, went in procession through the town. The strength of feeling can be gauged from the fact that clergy from the other two churches then joined the clergy of St Stephen in a satire mocking the bishop who had tried to suppress the feast along with his two most ardent supporters from among the canons. Following a letter from the bishop to the Archbishop of Sens, Charles VII decided to involve the secular authorities in making sure that good order was henceforth maintained.

It is likely that the problems at Troyes caused the chapter at Sens to review their own feast, as in 1444 it was provided that everything had to be conducted according to the book, with reverence and in good order. There were to be no disorderly crowds, discordant singing or mockery and the robes of the participants were to be those prescribed. However, one of the provisions gives a vivid idea of how riotous the proceedings had been. The participants were forbidden from throwing more than one bucket of water over the elected Lord in the cloisters on the eve of St John and no more than three buckets of water over him at Vespers on the feast of the Circumcision. It appears that this was allowed in case the Lord of the Feast might come to think that he was worthy of complete respect; moreover it would allow the real precentor to witness the humiliation of his rival.[9]

A selection of accounts from other cathedrals will provide examples of equally rowdy, violent and sacrilegious behaviour.

In Noyon, in 1419, one of the canons was disciplined for removing the sceptre from the altar in an attempt to revive the Feast which had been banned; and although it was later revived there were no longer to be any disreputable and scandalous songs, nor shameless words; and singing and dancing before the great door were also forbidden.

We have already seen that a chaplain was imprisoned in Laon for throwing fire from a gate towards the Patriarch of Fools.

At Antibes the ceremonies were more irreverent than anything else but they continued in the Franciscan church until 1645. Here the lay brothers and others, but not friars, indulged in a farcical performance of the liturgy by wearing vestments inside out, inverting books, using rounds of orange peel for spectacles, blowing the ash from the thurible into each other's faces and chanting nonsense.

At Rheims there was a sort of dramatic battle, where in response to the vicars and members of the choir mocking the clothing of the wealthier townsfolk, the law clerks retaliated with farses directed at the Church.

There were raucous celebrations at Chalôns-sur-Marne. The Bishop of Fools came in procession mounted on an ass accompanied by bells and music to a banquet prepared by the chapter before the great porch. Members of the lower clergy sang gibberish with grimaces in the cathedral itself. Then after another procession, dancing and a ball game, a crowd appeared before the cathedral making a dreadful noise with kettles and pans while the cathedral clergy came out in grotesque costumes and the bells were rung.

In Chartres the Pope of Fools, as well as indulging in other forms of unacceptable behaviour, demanded fines from those passing in the street. The situation in Auxuerre was even worse, for not only was the ringing of the bells a cause of nuisance but copes were seized as forfeits for contributions, and both men and women were attacked in the streets.

The problems at Tournai originated not so much from among the clergy but from the wealthy young men of the town. According to custom, the vicars of Notre Dame had to select one of their own to act as their Bishop of Fools on Holy Innocents' Day. In 1489 Matthieu de Porta was taken into the church and insulted there. The result was that the vicars were forbidden from holding their feast and the town forbidden from forcing an election. Despite there being peace for some years, the young men continued to feel resentful at the removal of their feast and so in

1498 they broke into the house of a chaplain and dragged him through the icy streets in a semi-dressed state to take part in the singing and dancing. Several other vicars were similarly treated but with a determination that can but be admired they all refused to take the part of Bishop of Fools. The complaints of the chapter falling on deaf ears, one of the vicars was chosen to be Bishop and at night by the light of the torches he had three buckets of water thrown over him to confirm his appointment. Subsequently he was dressed in a surplice and paraded through the town. They then discarded him and elected a clerk as Bishop. Because they bore a grudge against the priest of La Madeleine, they forced him out of the church during the Vespers of Epiphany and imprisoned him. The result was that the festival was abolished in 1500.

Perhaps the most serious disorder recorded was in Fréjus where a riot was instigated in 1558 by an attempt to suppress the feast. This led to the bishop, who had been threatened with murder, going into hiding while the mob attacked his palace.

Disturbances and irreverence also featured in the Spanish celebrations which were not necessarily those solely connected with the Feast of Fools, for it appears that in Spain the problems extended to other festivals as well.[10] The Third Council of Toledo in 589 ordered people to be mindful of the offices of the Church and not to disturb the worship of the monks by dances and vulgar ballads. This, however, was only part of the story, for in later years the liturgical dramas promoted by the clergy had degenerated to such an extent that there were constant complaints from the bishops about performances that were typified by buffoonery and coarseness, where even priests disguised themselves as scoundrels, killers, clowns and whores. The mixture of the sacred and profane was often a cause of scandal. Attempts to suppress these activities achieved only limited success, for D Alonso el Sabio in the Laws of the *Partidas* tried to prohibit priests from taking part in games of mockery, especially in churches. The Council of Toledo in 1473 found it necessary to forbid women called *soldaderas* from going publicly into the houses of prelates to feast and hold crude and evil conversations, flying in the face of decency by showing off and boasting. In addition there were theatrical performances, singing, dancing and other buffoonery which had to be suppressed in some of the cathedrals; but as in France, the abuses proved very difficult to control. In 1490 the Archbishop of Seville, in a decision confirmed in 1512 by a provincial council, ordered churches to be closed at night so as to prevent eating, drinking, secular songs and dances, adultery and fornication taking place on the vigils of the saints. An exemption was made for the feast of St Agosto which could be celebrated but without any of the previous indecencies, under pain of fines. The fact the council deemed it necessary to endorse the Archbishop's order suggests how hard the festivities were to control. Other attempts at suppression were made in Guadix and Baeza 1554, and again by the Archbishop of Seville in 1575. Attempts at suppression were complicated in the fifteenth and sixteenth centuries by a renewed interest in liturgical drama, backed by the monarchy and ecclesiastical authorities. Again, these often turned into farses and improper dances, and had to be controlled.

The degree of scurrilous behaviour is indicative of how the nature of the celebrations of the Feast of Fools differed from those of the Boy Bishop. Being adult celebrations, with young men the principal participants, they bore a more anti-authoritarian and hooligan aspect. It is these young men of the cathedral who seem to cause the authorities the most difficulties from year to year. There were, of course, abuses in the Boy Bishop celebrations to be dealt with, but where serious problems did arise during these celebrations, they were easier to control than those arising from the Feast of Fools; and in any event it was young men who were more often than not at the root, rather than the boys themselves.

All this explains why various councils, synods and chapters were so keen to control and suppress the Feast while viewing the Boy Bishop ceremonies with a more kindly spirit. Though the authorities were often willing to tolerate, or at least "turn a blind eye to", some high spirited celebrations, obviously many aspects of the Feast of Fools had to be curbed in order to secure reverence in worship, people's safety and their freedom from insulting activities.

Of course, the church authorities were wrestling with an age-old problem. If their efforts seem by turns strange, overbearing and ineffective, it is well to remember that even today we encounter the same problems of controlling the behaviour of young men who wish to indulge in violent or anti-social behaviour.

9

The Revival

The burgeoning interest in the Catholic heritage of the Church of England in the nineteenth century, which found expression in the Tractarian and Oxford Movements, provided a platform for the examination of the ancient liturgies of England and of medieval Catholic Europe, resulting in some pressure for the restoration, or partial restoration of the Sarum Use. Some within the Catholic Church also sought ways in which at least some of the features of this Use could be incorporated into building and liturgy, most famously A W N Pugin. The desire for a resurgence of the Boy Bishop in the twentieth century was born from the academic research into such liturgies. The modern Boy Bishop usually serves a somewhat different purpose from his medieval forebear with realigned and reinvented liturgies. While these new approaches undoubtedly serve a serious purpose, one tailored for the present age, it is also easy to detect in some more than hint of the medieval and the desire to present the sights, sounds, and atmosphere of that long past time. Yet, it is difficult to generalise since the revivals have each tended to follow their own course, dictated by the circumstances of the particular cathedral or church. Reference to the ancient liturgies can be found in each one but there lacks the coherence found in all the medieval liturgies of the Boy Bishop. Thus, the liturgies that we find today represent rather the flowering of individual creativity than a desire for a fuller recreation of the past or a desire for a common liturgy.

The reasons behind this are probably largely to do with the shades of churchmanship to be found within the Anglican Church – the more high church element being prepared to adopt an approach closer to the original – while others see it as some sort of counterpart to the May Queen. A further factor which seems to have influenced how far the ancient liturgies have been adhered to is the level of confidence that the church has in endeavouring to seek out a medieval past in the face of a world that often uses the term "medieval" as one of abuse.

Although most of the revivals have been within the Church of England, the Catholic Church, too, has revived the Boy Bishop in a number of places, but apparently with the same lack of liturgical conformity.

The first revivals

In the first half of the twentieth century an Anglican clergyman, Desmond Morse-Boycott, founded St Mary-of-the-Angels Choir School, independent of any single church. In this school, famous in its day, Morse-Boycott developed a version of the Chylde Bishop, as he preferred to call him, which included many of the elements later to be found in other places. He even wrote *The Boy Bishop Book* [1] complete with photographs, which includes not only the liturgy as it was used in the school, but also comments on the ceremony, and a brief (if somewhat generalised) history.

In this version, which has resonances of the medieval liturgies, on 6th December, the boy robed in amice, alb, girdle and sanctuary slippers, and having previously made his confession, was led to kneel before the altar while an anthem was played or a hymn sung. The boy, who appears to have been elected by fellow members of the choir, was presented as a worthy candidate by his Boy Chaplain. The beginning of the *sealing* [2] was a set of questions to be answered by the boy, to ascertain that he wished to be Chylde Bishop and to elicit promises about his conduct.

> *Wilt thou observe the rules of the office, be diligent in service and virtuous in conduct, both in public and in private?*

A set of prayers followed which included *Out of the mouths of babes and sucklings*, and then in another surprising departure seven boys from the choir in turn laid their hands on the boy's head, announcing *"N. or M., our Chylde Bishop"*, mirroring a real bishop's consecration. Another such mirroring came after with the singing of *Veni Creator*, an invocation of the Holy Spirit. After the boy was vested with each robe, the rings and the pectoral cross, a prayer relevant to each item was said, although, strangely, no mention of the crozier was made at this point. After a procession to the outside of the building, the doors were shut and the Boy Bishop struck the doors with his crozier three times to gain entry. Next, seated on a throne before the altar, the Boy Bishop received homage from all the other boys who approached with three genuflections, kissed his hand and gave a money-offering, with psalm 22, a hymn or

Morse Boycott investing a Chylde Bishop

instrumental piece either accompanying or following. When he had blessed the incense, the boy intoned the *Magnificat* and censed the altar; and after returning to his throne was himself censed before the censing of the choir and congregation. Following two prayers provision was made for the hymn *Once in Royal David's City* which was sometimes sung by the rest of boys holding candles and circling the Boy Bishop, or for the school song, without the aforementioned ceremonial. After the sermon and the blessing the boy passed through the church blessing people and receiving more homage and alms at the door. He held his office until Holy Innocents' Day, being accorded the privilege of singing Matins and Evensong daily and of signing his name with an X in the manner of a true bishop. At Evensong on Holy Innocents' Day he was silently disrobed before the altar, received a blessing and was rewarded with a glass of wine, a morsel of bread and a golden guinea.

Morse-Boycott saw the Boy Bishop as important in representing the significance and sanctity of the priesthood, hoping that many of the boys in his school would later become clergymen themselves. At least one did. At any rate, he noted that the boys took it all very seriously and that the Boy Bishop exhibited exemplary school conduct for the duration of his reign. Morse-Boycott was enough of a schoolmaster to accept that the criteria for choosing a boy should not be that he has exhibited *excellent* conduct; after all, he was seeking a *"Prince of Scholars, not a prig"*, yet he also recognised that the choice needed to be carefully made so that the boy chosen would not be likely to indulge in seriously bad behaviour. Ever a realist, he did, however, concede that it was impossible to determine this.

> *Not that such a child really exists, for work among boys is like building a beautiful garden on the edge of a volcano.*

Therefore, he does suggest that to some extent the secret ballot on 5th December was "rigged" because, in an echo of medieval York, and with an eye to practicality, the Principal and his staff would nominate certain boys, who would not only satisfy the requirements as to behaviour, but possess good enough voices and be able to fit the robes. Perhaps Morse-Boycott remembered roughly similar stipulations in medieval York. The runner up in the election was to act as chaplain with the promise of a half-guinea reward.

Directly or indirectly, this Liturgy proved to be an inspiration for many subsequent Liturgies which have included the Boy Bishop's promises and prayers offered at his robing.

There is a brief newsreel of these ceremonies, but it does not seem to give a very faithful account. Probably in order to save the expense of lighting the church, the Boy is robed at the church door in a very truncated ceremony.

However, influential as Morse-Boycott's version of the Boy Bishop was, there seem to have been at least two earlier revivals. One of these is recorded in a photograph at St Editha's, Tamworth, c.1923/4. Here the boy is pictured outside the main entrance to the church flanked by his two deacons, who wear their dalmatics over their surplices, and surrounded by what seems to be the choir. The other was even earlier. The ceremonies were introduced to St Nicholas, Berden in 1901 by the then vicar, Herbert Hudson, who formed the Guild of St Nicholas. The boys were elected by ballot and robed by Hudson himself as part of a miracle play. The first Boy Bishop was the vicar's son, Aelfric. One of the privileges enjoyed by the Boy Bishop was to accompany the vicar and the May Queen on a rare visit to the top of the church tower at 6.00 a.m. on May Day to appreciate the view. The Boy, having held his office for a year, became the cross bearer to his successor. Although the ceremonies were discontinued in 1937, they were revived 1955-1956 and again 1961-1966. There is some Pathé footage of the 1921 ceremony and the Gaumont Graphic Film Unit made film of the Boy's installation in the early 1930s.

There are other parishes that revived the Boy Bishop at about the same time. Mervyn Stockwood, who later became a very well-known figure as Bishop of Southwark, used a Boy Bishop liturgy when he was vicar of St Matthew's, Moorfields in Bristol. Here the boy, elected by the children of the parish, held office for the whole year, conducted the junior services every Sunday, and preached to the children twice a year. Stockwood made the particular point that he did not feel bound by the customs of the Middle Ages and was, therefore, free to introduce innovations.

Other places included Rotherhithe; St Michael's in Little Ilford; St Michael's, Romford Road, Manor Park, London; St Paul's Covent Garden (for which there was a picture in *The Church Times*, 27th December, 1968 of the Boy Bishop being greeted by members of the choir wearing Eton collars and saluting with top hats); St Christopher's, Scunthorpe; St Luke's, Mestycroft; St James the Greater, Pokesdown, Bournemouth; and Norton Parish Church, Sheffield. In Norton parish church the boy presided over a Whit-Monday observance, held office for a year, and in 1949 had a meeting with the Boy Bishop from Mestycroft. Morse-Boycott declined a meeting proposed for 1951 between the Norton boy and the boy from St Mary-of-the-Angels on the grounds that Whit Monday was not the traditional day.

Not that the Boy Bishops had it all their own way. A letter from Viner Hall published in the Weston-Super-Mare Gazette, 6th January 1945, criticising the Moorfields' Boy Bishop, is typical of the more extreme Protestant response.

> *For an irresponsible boy of 15 to be allowed to officiate publicly as if he were a priest of God; to pray and make supplication to the Lord of Heaven and Earth; and above all, with the approval of the Church is as blasphemous act of presumption as was the offering of strange fire by Nabdab and Abihu (Lev 10:1-11)*

Revivals in the 1970s and 1980s

The Boy Bishop at Hereford Cathedral is probably the most famous of the modern revivals. The cathedral hopes that at the heart of this liturgy the *"same, profound, Gospel of Truth"* concerning *"humility and belonging to the Kingdom of God"* will be symbolised.

> *Deep in Christianity there is not only the expectation that sometimes the down-trodden come out on top and "the mighty are cut down", but also the teaching that children are nothing less than the measure of man.*

The boy is usually appointed by the Master of Choristers and then given spiritual instruction by one the Cathedral clergy because of the spiritual demands made upon him. By the time of his enthronement he is expected to have gained some knowledge of the liturgy, which includes the correct method for censing the altar. Canon Iles in *Another Winter's Tale* [3] (1986) understood the need to reconcile the medieval world with the modern.

> *Some colourful, medieval pageantry is still valuable in our lives, not as a relic from by-gone days, but as an opportunity to re-open well-tried routes to meaning. The subtle blend of earthiness and spirituality, of extravaganza and sanctity, which it contains is not easy for twentieth century people to understand and appreciate. But if we handle the mixture with discretion and some careful re-*

direction, it still brings insights into God and human life which are
too precious to lose.

The Boy Bishop liturgy, which is inserted into Evensong, begins with the entry of the choir and the Boy Bishop singing *Sedentem*. Once they are in their places in the choir, the preces and responses for Evensong are sung, followed by a psalm and the lesson, 1 Kings 3:1-10, concerning the call of the child Samuel to the service of God. The processional route is via the north choir aisle to the Lady Chapel, returning by the south choir aisle, but with the true bishop remaining on his throne. On the return of the procession to the choir, the bishop leaves his throne and stands on the steps of the sanctuary with the Boy Bishop and his assistants in front of him. The Boy Bishop reaffirms his baptismal and confirmation promises to the bishop and undertakes to pray for all members of the Cathedral Foundation and all in need of his prayers. The Boy Bishop prays for the strength of the Holy Spirit and is blessed by the bishop who hands over his staff and announces the Boy Bishop to the people. As the beginning of the *Magnificat* is sung, the Boy Bishop goes to the altar rail and at the *Deposuit* takes the bishop's throne. From the throne, holding the pastoral staff, he gives the blessing. Evensong then proceeds as normal until the Boy Bishop goes to the high altar to receive two pence as a token of the two pence that his predecessors received for the purchase of candles to be used by the choristers. Evensong concludes without the blessing since it was given earlier. In the same way that in the Middle Ages the Boy Bishop's offerings had been diverted to support the choristers' education, the collection is used to support the Chorister Bursary Endowment Fund.

Although Salisbury Cathedral possesses some of the most precise detail about the Boy Bishop liturgies in its medieval documents, the current Boy Bishop ceremony is based to a large extent on the revived Hereford Use. Here the Boy Bishop is not elected as such but is the boy who holds the position of Bishop's Chorister, whose role by a historical quirk has sometimes been regarded as a remnant of the medieval Boy Bishop. At Evensong the preces and responses are followed as usual by the psalm, the same lesson as at Hereford and a hymn. The Boy Bishop's promises follow the Hereford pattern as does his prayer for strength, after which he is blessed by the bishop. In addition to the usual episcopal insignia the bishop gives the Boy a book of prayers. Having preached his sermon, he receives the customary two pence. There then follows a hymn and the *Magnificat*, during which he takes the bishop's throne. Afterwards, as at Hereford, he gives his blessing. Evensong concludes in the usual way.

St John's C of E First School, Dorking where the Boy Bishop was elected from those in year 3, held the ceremonies from 1970 until 1987, using a form of liturgy adapted from St Mary-of-the-Angels, with the additional responsibility given to the Boy of reading the epistle during the Eucharist on the last day of the Autumn term. The school closed in the summer of 1988.

The most detailed and authentic of these revivals began in 1984 at St Paul's, Wokingham. However, the approach that guided the revival here was not principally medieval in focus but perhaps more in line with present day concerns, and so the role of children within the Divine Scheme was emphasised. To give this a more practical application the offerings to the Boy Bishop were not to be assigned to his use. Instead, each family attending the ceremonies was asked to bring a new toy or gift token to be presented to the Boy Bishop and then sent to the Church of England Children's Society (now called the Children's Society). The evening of the Second Sunday in Advent was deemed the most suitable date for the ceremony, despite lack of any historical precedent, for the purely practical reason that this did

The Boy Bishop Ceremonies at St. Paul's, Wokingham

not clash with any other Advent activities, while it allowed sufficient time for the Society to process the gifts ready for Christmas. The emphasis laid upon the high purpose of the ceremony was from the outset calculated to circumvent any suggestion of mere play-acting and the ceremonies were always presented with the same seriousness as any other liturgy of the Church. Elections were never held, the Boy being selected in alternate years from the choir and serving team by the choirmaster and head server. The Boy was trained for about four weeks in singing, the ceremonial (including censing the altar) and how to lead the Liturgy. The rector also guided the Boy in his spiritual responsibilities. The specific connection with children was strengthened as the money for the Boy Bishop's robes and those of his deacons was donated by parents as a memorial for their dead child; and the ring was purchased from money given for the same purpose by a second set of parents.

The complete altar serving team of MC (master of ceremonies), thurifer, acolytes, crucifer, boat boy, two bishops' assistants and two deacons was composed of children, except for the MC, who was on hand in case of emergencies. Seven other children were nominated to bring up the episcopal robes and insignia. The ceremonies themselves were embedded in Evensong, which followed a more-or-less standard pattern until after the *Magnificat* and the sermon. The responsory *These were redeemed* was sung by the choir and followed by a prayer. After the Boy made his promises to the rector, kneeling before him on the chancel step, he was invested with his robes and instruments of office. Standing in front of the people he was acclaimed with *These were redeemed* and *Sedentem*, to which he sang the plainchant response *"Rejoice in the Lord, O ye righteous: and be ye lift up, all ye that are pure of heart"*. During *Once in Royal David's City* the procession went to the Lady Chapel where the boy censed the altar, accompanied by the choir singing *Alma Redemptoris Mater*. When the procession had returned to the chancel steps the Boy Bishop led the people in three prayers and the *Pater Noster*. While the gifts for the Society were presented, a further hymn was sung and the ceremonies concluded with the Boy Bishop's blessing. The duties of the Boy Bishop did not end here, however. He undertook to pray daily for the parish during the period of his reign, to lead the sacristy prayers after Mass and Evensong, to set an example to the other youngsters and to preach a sermon on the Sunday next before Candlemas. He was allowed to wear his pectoral cross – and, if a chorister, his purple cassock, too – during all services from his investiture until Candlemas when, after being dressed once more in his robes and assisting with the distribution of candles and then leading the sacristy prayers for a final time, his duties ended. The Boy Bishop's Deacons were customarily chosen from the ranks of previous Boy Bishops. The boys who took the role of Boy Bishop all demonstrated a deepening spiritual awareness and maturity, and never was there any hint of jealousy from among their peers. Correspondingly the boys never felt ridiculous or childish and parents never viewed the ceremonies simply as an opportunity of dressing up their little boys in a cute costume; it was all too serious for that. The popularity was overwhelming from the first revival: congregations of three to four hundred – almost as many as for Christmas itself – and mountains of gifts that hardly fitted on the chancel step. The names of the Boy Bishops are listed in a frame next to the frame naming all the rectors of the parish. The ceremonies, however, now seem to have been abandoned.

The Boy Bishop was revived in St Mary's Mendlesham in 1981 following the request of a young boy for there to be a special job for boys. The enthronement takes place at the Sung Mass on the Sunday closest to St Nicholas's Day. One boy acts as chaplain and other children present the robes and insignia. The ceremony follows a simple pattern of promises, robing and enthronement. In the afternoon, the Boy Bishop and his chaplain collect the gift envelopes for the Children's Society, give out Christingles and join the procession around the church. He has the further task of lighting the candles on the Advent wreath. He is given a special place at the Christmas Eve carol service, on Christmas Day and at Epiphany. His final duty of distributing a book to each child in the congregation on behalf of the Sunday School completed, he resigns his office on 13th January, the Baptism of Christ.

The Boy Bishop of St John the Baptist, Claines, Worcester has a pedigree stretching back to 1971. This Boy Bishop, chosen from the choir by the churchwarden, has the unusual distinction of carrying the Claines Crosier, which incorporates the silver head of a medieval crosier found in Claines in the 1940s and given to the then Bishop of Worcester. The Boy Bishop's duties include attending carol services at Claines School and Alice Ottley School, a pilgrimage to Shrewsbury Abbey, accompanying home sick communions, daily readings and prayers, a sermon and a visit to the grave of the 12th Boy Bishop who died in 1984, two years after his reign.

In the parish of North Walsham the Boy Bishop, who is invested during the Communion Service, leads parts of the liturgy and preaches a sermon. In a reversal of the medieval tradition, at the end of the liturgy, he offers golden coins to the children of the parish. Naturally his largesse is limited; the coins are merely chocolate covered in foil.

The Boy Bishop in modern times, like his medieval counterpart, has been winged across the Atlantic. In the Episcopal Cathedral of All Saints in Albany, New York, the liturgy followed a familiar pattern: the presentation of the Boy, the Boy's promises, the prayer *Out of the mouths of babes and sucklings*, the blessing of the Boy, the robing with prayers at each item, a final prayer and the Boy Bishop's blessing. These ceremonies which began in 1979 lasted for over twenty years before being discontinued.

Other places include:

St Katharine, Southbourne, Dorset
St Nicholas Newchurch-in-Rossendale (1957-1975)
St Christopher, Southbourne
St John, Woodley
St Nicholas, Tuxford
St Mary Edwinstowe (girl Child Bishops from 1980)
St William of York, Reading

Unfortunately, in some of these places the Boy Bishop has faded away once more.

Later revivals

Westminster (Catholic) Cathedral revived their Boy Bishop in 2006, with boys chosen from the choir school. The method of selection is somewhat unusual, for the boys in the top year submit sermons, the precentor deciding the winning entry. The boy is invested on 12th March, the old feast day of St Gregory and the school's patronal festival. After Mass the Boy comes forward and, following the celebrant's prayer, he is robed in cope and mitre. The Headmaster of the Choir School reads a lesson (Job 32:6,9) before the Boy preaches his sermon, leads a final prayer and gives his blessing. A revival of sorts had been attempted in the early part of the twentieth century when, to commemorate St Aloysius, there was an annual procession of children, and a sermon from the top step of the high altar preached by a boy, dressed in cassock and biretta and surrounded by his attendants.

In the parish of St Nicholas, Longparish, the primary school celebrates the Boy Bishop in the church on the afternoon of St Nicholas's Day. The Boy is chosen by the staff. The first Boy Bishop was installed by the Archdeacon of Winchester. The liturgy, which is fairly simple, has the following form: prayer, hymn, reading (Luke

6:36-38), talk, installation and enthronement, prayer, hymn, and a blessing given by the rector and the Boy Bishop. At the end of the ceremony, the Boy Bishop gives out chocolate coins to all the children.

At All Saints' Church, in Wellingborough, where the ceremonies were revived in 2008, the Bishop of Brixworth installed the first Boy Bishop. Here the Boy Bishop leads prayers on certain days and preaches a sermon during the carol service.

Later revivals elsewhere in England:

Newcastle Cathedral
St Andrew, Chinnor
St George the Martyr, Waterlooville
Wymondham Abbey
St Nicholas, Tuxford (revived again in 2002, first girl bishop 2003)
St Nicholas, Gosforth
St John the Evangelist, Clevedon
St Nicholas, Alcester
St Nicholas, Newchurch-in-Rossendale (revived again in 2007)
St John the Evangelist, Forton, Gosport (a Girl Bishop preaching a month of sermons)
St Nicholas Ecumenical Parish, Warndon Villages
Oldham Parish Church
All Saints, Putney Common, London

Later revivals in other parts of the world:

St Mark's Portobello, Edinburgh
Arrasate, Spain
Burgos, Spain
Burriana, Spain
Legazpia, Spain
Palencia, Spain
Segura, Spain
Zegama, Spain
Graz, Austria
Chavagnes International College, Chavanges-en-Paillers, France

Wichern-Schule das Rauhe Haus, Hamburg, Germany
Magdala Parish, Ottstedt, Germany
St John's Anglican Church, East Malvern, Australia
Our Lady of Mount Carmel School, Waterbury, Connecticut, USA
St Peter's Episcopal Church, Cazenovia, New York, USA (Boy and Girl Bishops)
Christ the King, Sharpsburg, Georgia, USA
St Nicholas Parish, Sunman, Indiana, USA
St Joseph's Catholic School, Greenville, South Carolina, USA
St Mary's Cathedral, Ogdensburg, New York, USA

These lists are by no means comprehensive and there may well be many more places where the ceremonies have been revived

The ceremonies at the Abbey of Montserrat strictly do not belong to the revivals as they seem to have been a continuous tradition. Here the celebrations begin on 22nd November, St Cecilia's Day,[4] when the Boy and his two assistants are selected after a set of elections. The Boy Bishop's duties last for one day when, dressed in episcopal robes and with ring and staff, he performs the offices for the day, preaches a sermon, chooses the day's menu for the whole community and indicates the pieces of music that will be played at the choir's concert. This concert, dedicated to the Boy Bishop, includes a song about the legend of St Nicholas. The ceremonies were surrounded with secrecy for many years, but in more recent times they have been filmed. Other places in Catalonia, usually monasteries and other religious communities, celebrate the Boy Bishop: Girona, Lleida and Vic.

Elsewhere in Spain, in the Basque country, the St Nicholas traditions have included very young boys of between about three and six years old. These Boy Bishops often distribute alms, ride horses (as in Safe) and preside over meals with priests or teachers. Sometimes they are accompanied by fellow pupils (as in Zegama) and receive treats of nuts, cakes and dried fruit. He is also said to survive in Palma de Mallorca.

The Sermons

As is to be expected, the sermons of the modern Boy Bishops bear little relation to the sermons preached in the sixteenth century. Gone is the attack, the hard-hitting humour, the depth, the challenge and the length. Today's sermons, naturally, reflect the world in which they are preached. The current trend is for the Boy to reflect on his own experience and response to the Faith, sometimes with a reference to Saint

Nicholas, and to give a simple moral message. The following is a fairly typical example, preached by an 11/12 year old at Wokingham.

In the name of the Father, the Son and the Holy Spirit.

> *Now that I am coming to the end of my term as Boy Bishop I would like to say how much I have enjoyed the job. Last year J. stood here on this box to preach a sermon to you all, so when the Rector asked me if I would like to do the same I said, "Yes." (I think now that I am beginning to regret it.) I might also say that my dear brother, the first Boy Bishop got away with this bit.*

> *Last week, the Rector came to our house to talk about today's sermon with me. (Mummy asked him to come as I was beginning to panic about it.) We talked about what a sermon is for and what I might put into it.*

> *He said that it was important that I understood what I was talking about, so I thought I would talk to you today about perseverance. (Don't worry! It's quite a short sermon.)*

> *When I was much younger, my brother began to play the cornet in the school band. When I got into the third form at ... I had the chance to start playing the same instrument, so I decided to give it a try. At first I got on quite well with it and practised every day – well almost! And found it very enjoyable. Unfortunately I was a bit impatient and was very disappointed that we were not playing in concerts, and gradually my practising became less and less until eventually I was not progressing. In fact, I was not really improving at all. You have probably guessed by now that I don't play the cornet any more and I must say that I regret not carrying on with it when I see the pleasure that my brother has playing in the various bands and orchestras that he does.*

> *Eventually, I left ....School and went to secondary school where I was introduced to rugby. I had never played rugby before, but I really love every minute of it, learning in lessons, learning new rules and playing with my school friends in a team.*

A Boy Bishop at St Paul's, Wokingham

I was lucky enough to be chosen to play for the school team, which meant that I had to go to rugby practice after school, so that we could practise moves, the secrets of scrimmaging, line outs, setting up rucks, etc. In the beginning we did not have much idea, but we have really improved (my Dad says) and have even won some matches which we wouldn't have done without practice, commitment and perseverance.

The reason that I have told you of my two contrasting experiences is that I think we can apply them to our Christian Faith. It is no good for us to come to church on Sunday and then think of ourselves as perfect Christians. We have to continually practise our beliefs in the way that we treat other people. We must always find time to say our prayers and continually try to live our lives in the way God wanted us to do so.

If we do not persevere in this way with our faith, it will wither away, just like my playing the cornet, and it will be to our lasting regret. Our faith should be like my rugby playing – something to be worked at, encouraged, practised and enjoyed.

In the name of the Father, the Son and the Holy Spirit. Amen.

This sermon certainly has charm, directness and a clearly discernable structure, even if it lacks the vigour and edge of those from the Middle Ages. This is one of the ways in which the Boy Bishop has acclimatised himself to the modern age.

The modern liturgies are child centred but in a different way from the medieval liturgies, and the message is subtlety different. Although both the medieval and modern liturgies remind people that the needs of children and their insights should never be neglected, the medieval emphasis on the innocence of the child as a model for moral behaviour, the attention given to the violence of the massacre of the Holy Innocents and the condemnatory tone of the sermons has just about completely disappeared. That is not to argue that either approach is to be preferred; all liturgies change and adapt to some degree. As far as the Boy Bishop is concerned, there is no reason why, after having been given a new lease of life, he should not reign under a new dispensation.

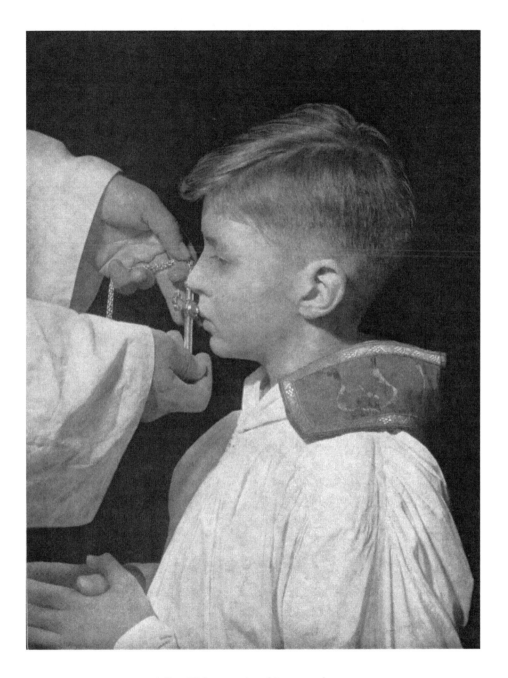

A Boy Bishop receives his pectoral cross

The first Boy Bishop at St Paul's, Wokingham

10

An Additional Chapter for Those Who Like Lists

Inventories

There are many inventories listing robes and other articles used in the Boy Bishop ceremonies which give an impression of how seriously the feast was regarded.[1] The splendid robes would have created a marvellous spectacle, especially in the great processions. These inventories are all the more remarkable when the cost of such elaborate vestments is calculated, this in an age when parishes often would not possess full sets of vestments for every season, and when the vicar and parish of Morebath in the sixteenth century had to save for years to afford a set of requiem Mass vestments.[2]

A fifteenth century roll printed in the notes to the Northumberland Household Book

Imprimis, i myter, well garneshed with perle and precious stones, with nowches of silver, and gilt before and behind.

Item, iiij rynges of silver and gilt, with four redde precious stones in them.

Item, i pontifical with silver and gilt, with a blew stone in hytt.

Item, i owche [brooch] broken, silver and gilt, with iiij precious stones, and a perle in the myddes.

Item a crosse, with a staf of coper and gilt, with the ymage of St Nicolas in the myddes.

Item, i vesture [set of vestments], redde, with lyons of silver, with brydds [birds] of gold in the orferes [decorative bands] of the same.

Item, i albe to the same with starres in the paro.

Item, i white cope, stayned with tristells and orferes [of] redde sylkes, with does of gold, and whytt napkins about ther necks

Item, iiij copes [of] blue silk, with red orferes, trayled with whitt braunches and flowers.

Item, i steyned cloth of the ymage of St Nycholas.

Item, i tabard of skarlet, and a hodde thereto, lyned with whitt sylk.

Item, a hode of skarlett, lyned with blue sylk.

Westminster Abbey

1388

A mitre decorated with gold, silver plates and several stones and with an image of St Nicholas on the front and *Ora Pro Nobis* embroidered on the back in pearls.

A staff with a silver and gold, and the images of Saints Peter and Edward the Confessor sitting upon thrones.

Two pairs of kid leather gloves with gold and silver plates and the inscription *Ora pro nobis beata Nicholae.*

A blood-coloured cope ornamented with gryphons and other beasts, and fountains.

A cope of ruby and blood-coloured velvet with gold embroidery and the new arms of England woven in to it.

A gold ring with a large sapphire, four pearls and eight small stones.

A rochet for the feast of St Nicholas.

A surplice for the feast of St Nicholas.

3 grey amices, one for the Boy Bishop.

2 albs.

A mitre, a pair of gloves and a ring were also listed as no longer used.

1540

The vj myter of Seynt Nycholas byssoppe, the grounde there of of whyte sylk, garnysshed complete with fflowres, gret and small, of sylver and gylte, and stones complete in them, with the scripture, *Ora pro nobis Sancte Nicholai*, embrodered theron in perll, the sydes sylver and gylt, and the toppys of sylver and gylt, and enamelyd with ij labelles of the same, and garnysshed in lyk maner, and with viij long bells of sylver and gylt, weying all together xxiij unces (This mitre seems to bear a close resemblance to the one listed in 1387. The same?)

The third Crose for Seynt Nycholas bysshope the hed therof sylver and gylt garnysshed with great perles and stonys haveing an ymage of Seynt Peter and an other of Seynt Edward of sylver and gylt, lacking vij stonys and perlys the staff therof round of coper and tymber weying all together lx unces. (The same staff as the one listed in 1388?)

a grete blewe clothe with Kyngs on horsse-bake for Saynt Nicholas cheyre [used as a canopy]

St Paul's Cathedral

1245

28 worn and shabby copes and mantles for the Feast of the Innocents and the Feast of Fools.

1295

A white mitre embroidered with flowers.

A pastoral staff with a copper gilt curve, and pommel with many vines and images for the boy bishop.

1402

2 staves for the Boy Bishop

London, St Benet-Fynck

A bishop Nicholas myter.

London, Elsing Hospital, Spital

A small cope for the Child Bishop.

London, St Katherine near the Tower

Saincte Nicholas cope.

London, St Mary-at-Hill

A myter for a Bishop of Seint Nycholas-tyde garnished with sylver and anelyed and perle and counterfete stones.

London, St Mary Woolnoth

The Bishopp's mytre garnyshed with silver, perles, and counterfett stones.

London, St Peter Cheap

1431
ij childes copes for St Nicholas, with j myter, j tonicle, j cheseble, and iij feble aubes for childer and a Crose for the bysshope.

London, Temple Church

1307
Two pairs of albes for boys.
Twenty-eight choral copes and four little copes for the choristers.

Cambridge, Great St Mary

1503
It., a crose and staffe for Seint Nicholas

1550 the parish sold the following:
It., ye rede cote and qwood yt St Nicholas dyd wer the color red.
It., the vestement and cope yt Seynt Nycholas dyd wer. Also albs for the children.

Evelyn-White also mentions a Boy Bishop's cope of white satin tissue, embroidered in floss silks, with buds, flowers, etc. that was exhibited at a meeting of the Archaeological Institute in 1861.

Durham Cathedral

xx copes with six tunicles for the children.

v albs for the children.

Exeter

An ivory staff and mitre

Hadleigh

1480

A chesible and a cope for St Nicholas.

Lichfield

1345

Four small choir copes for the choristers on Holy Innocents' Day.

In the fifteenth century
mitre.
cope.
gloves.
sandals.
staff.

Lincoln

1536

a coope of Rede velvet with rolles and clowdes ordeyned for the barne bisshop with this scriptur *the hye wey ys best.*

Lincoln, St Christopher

1488

Item, a cope of clothe of golde ffeeble for the childe Bisshop.
Item, a cope ffeble for a childe of dyvers colours, and iij copes of white bustyan and the orpharies of grene, these iij copies being small coopes for children.
Item, ij awbes of say for children of oon sewte.

North Elmham

1547
It'm for making of ye Chyldren's Coopes…xvj d.

Norwich

1498
Gloves were bought for the Boy Bishop

1506
A robe of worsted linen, with purple satin in honour of St Nicholas, for the Boy Bishop, to be worn day and night on St Nicholas's Day, within the parish of St-Martin-at-the-Palace-Gates, was left in will.

Norwich, St Andrew's

In the reign of Edward VI
Robes for the Boy Bishop.

Norwich, St Peter Mancroft

1368
A set of silk vestments: one chasuble, two tunicles, one cope and three albs
An expensive mitre and pastoral staff.

Oxford, All Souls'

i chasuble
i cope and mitre

Oxford, St Frideswide

In the reign of Henry VIII for the choristers

Tunicles of red and white damask and silk.

Blue and white amices of richly brocaded silk and chequered with red silk and gold.

Albs

Oxford, St Mary Magdalen College

1495

For the boys:
Red, white and crimson tunicles with damask and velvet orphreys.
One set of blue damask albs, and two with silk apparels.
A banner of St Nicholas.

Rotherham

Myter for the barne-bishop of cloth of gold, with two knoppes of silver, gilt and enamelled.

Salisbury

1222

A gold ring for the Feast of the Boys.

Sandwich, St Mary

A lytyll chesebyll for seynt Nicholas bysschop.

Winchester College

A mitre of cloth of gold with trappings of silver gilt and a pastoral staff of copper gilt.

1421

A cross of gold and copper with a staff *pro Episcopo puerorum*

Witchingham

1556

A St Nicholas cope.

Wykeham's College, Oxford

A richly brocaded, embroidered, silk mitre.

York Minster

One cope *de tissue pro Episcopo puerorum.*
Nine copes for the boys.
A ring for the *Episcopus puerorum.*
Two brooches.

France, Bayeux

Two mitres (one richly embroidered with four images, a pastoral staff, gloves.
Four copes for the choir.

Spain, Lérida

Fifteenth century
Mitre.
Ring.

Some other places in the Middle Ages that celebrated the Boy Bishop not mentioned elsewhere in this book, for which there is some information

Aberdeen Grammar School[3]
Antwerp – Edward III made a donation of 23s 6d[4].
Barcelona[5]
Besançon[6]
Bourges[7]
Brussels[8]
Bury St Edmunds[9] – a very brief description of the liturgy

Cambridge, King's College[10] – The Boy Bishop to officiate on 6th December as at Eton.

Canterbury Grammar School[11] – no Boy Bishop in 1464

Canterbury, St Peter[12]

Châlons-sur-Saône[13] – a brief description of the boys changing stalls and the procession in 1624.

Erlyngham[14] – had a copy of the Boy Bishop liturgy as performed at Salisbury.

Gerona, church of St Felix[15] – had an *abbatellus*, a rival to the Boy Bishop of the cathedral.

Granada[16]

Grenoble[17]

Hamburg[18] – A Boy Abbot elected on St Andrew's Day who gave way to Boy Bishop on St Nicholas's Day.

Heton[19] – King Edward I's gift in 1299.

Holyrood Abbey[20] (and elsewhere in Scotland) James IV's gifts to Boy Bishops of Holyrood Abbey and St Giles.

Lima[21] – A Council of Lima 1567 suppressed the ceremony of the *episcopolum*.

London, Lambeth[22] – 1523 payment.

London, St Stephen's Chapel[23] – payment by Henry VI.

London, King's Chapel at Westminster[24] – payment by Queen Elizabeth of York, 1502.

Louth[25] – payements in 1500, 1501, 1505.

Lyons[26] – brief note on the liturgy

Malaga[27] – brief description of the ceremonies and reform.

Mosburg[28]

Nantes[29]

New Romney[30]

Northampton[31]

Norwich, St Martin in the Plains[32]

Norwich, St Peter-per-Mountergate[33]

Nottingham[34] – a gift from the king.

Palencia[35]

Perpignan[36]

Prague[37]

Roye[38] – some notes about the liturgy, reform and interruptions.

Rumsey[39] – nuns' celebration.

St Albans[40]

Salamanca[41]

Seo de Urgel[42]

Soissons[43]

Troyes[44] – Boy Bishop allowed with conditions.

Valencia[45]

Vich[46]

Wells[47]

Worcester, St Nicholas[48]

Zaragoza[49]

Zug[50] – Boy Bishop with military bodyguard levied taxes on stalls and booths at the fair.

11

Endnote

The ceremonies of the Boy Bishop reveal some of the contradictions and tensions in medieval society, in fact the sort of contradictions and tensions that are found in all societies. The Middle Ages in Europe was no different from any other period of history in that it was not completely homogeneous in its outlook, tempting as it sometimes is to regard it as such. Its heterogeneity sprang not only from a lively spirit of enquiry, interest in the classical world and contact with other continents and civilisations, but also from the obvious fact that a period spanning hundreds of years must of necessity have been forced to evolve new ideas if it were not to fossilise.

Underlying the perennial antipathy between the purists and the liberals there are to be found many more such interesting cross-currents revealed by the Boy Bishop ceremonies, which, for convenience sake, might be illustrated in the form of a number of apparent contradictions.

One important question, which in post-Reformation days resolved itself into part of the conflict between Protestantism and Catholicism, was the place of seriousness and enjoyment in religious worship. On the one hand, it could be pointed out that the worship of the Divine ought to be accompanied by appropriate solemnity and earnestness of mind. Yet, did this provide sufficient reason to rule out celebration and fun, especially if this could bring people to a closer understanding of the Church's teachings? The cathedrals and churches stand witness to a less than serious approach in their ornamentation, particularly in such features as gargoyles and other carvings in wood and stone which often illustrate the more vigorous humour of the age. In the Middle Ages the two attitudes of mind coexisted under the broad roof of the Catholic Church, and the determined opposition to the sporadic efforts to restrain, reform and suppress the ceremonies of the Boy Bishop provide evidence for this.

The ceremonies could be viewed both as expressions of reverence for the clergy and of a particular type of anti-clericism. The more Protestant elements within the Church of England traditionally held the over-simplified view that the ceremonies were a typical piece of Popish mummery combined with Romish priestcraft. Of course, the very act of a boy impersonating a bishop tends to presuppose a reverence for that office, especially if the boy's actions copy those of the legitimate prelate; and even more so if the forms of worship are designed to impress upon the people the dignity of the boy in occupying that position. Yet the process of unseating the clergy and replacing them by boys, the penalties that were exacted against unworthy clergy and religious in some places and the more undignified elements that were sometimes introduced into the worship itself argue a more complex relationship with the clergy. Undoubtedly, the Boy Bishop ceremonies could express dissatisfaction with the behaviour and status of the clergy. As the clergy were not universally admired and respected the ceremonies could at times become tinged with anti-clercism, especially on the continent. We should, nevertheless, probably be mistaken if we were to regard these ceremonies as a challenge to the Church or as an unwelcome concession to the more vulgar elements of society. They may have been too ostentatious for our taste but the spirit that motivated them was decidedly benign.

The Church of the Middle Ages is seen as a particularly hierarchical institution. On earth the Pope was the pinnacle of the authoritarian pyramid that stretched down through the bishops, priests, deacons, subdeacons and lower clergy, with the laity at the base. Nonetheless, it was not solely an authoritarian hierarchy: consultation did play a role within the decision-making processes as, for instance, the constitutions of cathedral chapters and monastic institutions show. The election of the Boy Bishop reveals one element of this political duality of thought with the more authoritarian element being the desire of some clergy to impose their own choices on the choristers.

Just as in the cult of Dionysus and in the Saturnalian celebrations classical civilisation had seen the need for the shackles of propriety and decency to be slackened, but held within the safety of a closely-ordered society watched over by Eunomia or Justitia, so a similar understanding underlies the medieval attitude to the Boy Bishop. The *Deposuit* and the some of the festivities, especially where they were influenced by the Feast of Fools, are symptomatic both of a belief in the ordered nature of creation and of the fear of chaos. The topsy-turvy nature of boys ruling men and of the plays and masques, shows a desire to escape from the rigid order of things, but in the medieval mind there was also a dread of chaos and a desire for order which found their expression in incorporating the Boy Bishop into the strictly defined ritual of the cathedral, so that the disorder might be symbolically controlled and not let loose with an anarchy that threatened to destroy society.

The Church itself was in an ambiguous position, often championing the cause of the poor and dispossessed and yet itself wielding immense temporal and spiritual power. Again, the *Deposuit* gave expression to the notion of the powerful giving way to the lowly; the adult clergy of all ranks were dispossessed, at least for a day by the least powerful members of the cathedral communities, the boys. In people's minds the high and the low did not operate in completely different spheres, although the class divisions were particularly inflexible; they belonged to the same continuum that might at any time be interrupted or shaken by Fate or Divine Providence. It was as well for all to note that status and power did not necessarily confer security.

Death was a regular visitor. It could take away the life of the newly-born or the adult with little warning. Its presence was far more keenly felt in the Middle Ages than today, for it struck frequently and often at random. While parents could expect to lose one or more of their children before they reached adulthood, there were likewise large numbers of children who had lost one or both parents. Even so, the dead, were not regarded as lost to the living; they were part of the Communion of Saints, constantly prayed for in requiem Masses and in other devotions for the departed, and recalled to mind by candles in churches. Therefore, the barrier between the world of the living and the dead was not absolute; and the saints, while on earth having provided examples of heroic virtue for the living, could further aid them with their prayers in the heavenly kingdom after their deaths. The Holy Innocents, so vividly brought to mind at the Christmas season, offered to medieval man both the virtues of their innocence and their powerful spiritual assistance in petitioning God.

If the medieval period was violent by our standards, it also recognised the virtues of innocence and purity. Some of the Boy Bishop celebrations were attended by violence and murder, and the martyrdom of the Innocents did provide medieval preachers with plenty of opportunities to dwell on gore, mutilation and violent death, but it was the triumphant purity of the slaughtered children and the glorious innocence of the Boy Bishop that were set before people as the icons of virtue. Thus it was that sin and righteousness could be juxtaposed in a shocking but memorable story. Mankind, ever likely to fall into sin, was given the opportunity to embrace virtue; society, with its many imperfections, could be given the grace to reform by answering the call to become pure.

The dichotomy between the secular and spiritual worlds was not as keenly felt in the Middle Ages as perhaps we perceive it to be in contemporary society. The Church authorities might in some places and at some times have been keen to extirpate the coarser secular influences from religious worship, but there would have been no sharp division between the two worlds. Religion not only formed the basis of society, it permeated it at every level and influenced to a profound extent the thoughts, daily routines, actions and decisions of its members. Correspondingly, society influenced the Church in myriad ways, from its administration to its music and liturgy. The two worlds tended to collide only when their interests clashed or when it was perceived that one was gaining disproportionate influence.

The ceremonies themselves provide examples of the tension between conformity and diversity. The liturgies across Europe show that the principal elements of the ceremonies were generally constant and that the underlying message to be communicated was the same. Despite this, there was a variation in the exact form of the liturgy, the ritual and the ceremonial, while the associated festivities assume an even wider variation. There was at one and the same time the desire of cathedrals and monasteries to be like their neighbours but also to mark things which made them distinctive. Hand in hand with this went the desire to conform to tradition and the desire to reform it: the desire to be in step with the past and the desire to discover new, better paths.

When reading about the past it is easy to be overwhelmed by a sense of the Other, a sort of romanticised recreation of history. Much about the Middle Ages is indeed different, but in very truth, the people of that age are more like us than we might care to admit.

Appendix A

Rex gloriose martyrum,
Corona confitentium,
Qui respuentes terrea
Perducis ad caelestia,
Aurem benignam protinus
Intende nostris vocibus;
Trophaea sacra pangimus,
Ignosce quod deliquimus.
Tu vincis inter Martyres
Parcisque Confessoribus;
Tu vince nostra crimina
Largitor indulgentiae.
Deo Patri sit Gloria
Et Filio, qui a mortuis,
Surrexit, ac Paraclito,
In sempiterna saecula.
Amen.

Sancti et justi in Domino gaudete, alleluia. Vos elegit Deus in hereditatem sibi. Alleluia.

O glorious king of martyrs,
The crown of confessors,
Who earthly things rejecting,
You lead to heaven.

Constantly lend your kind ear
To our voices.
We sing of their sacred trophies;
Forgive us because we fail.

You conquer among the martyrs
And you spare the confessors.
Overcome our sins;
Give generous pardon.
Glory be to God the Father
And to the Son, who rose from the dead,
And to the Holy Spirit (Paraclete),
Throughout all ages.
Amen.

O Saints and the Just rejoice in the Lord. Alleluia.
God selected you into his inheritance for himself. Alleluia

Appendix B

Celsa pueri concrepent melodia,
Eia, Innocentum colentes tripudia,
Quos infans Christus hodie vexit ad astra.
Quos trucidavit frendens insania
Herodianae fraudis, ob nulla crimina,
In Bethlehem ipsius cuncta et per confinia,
A bimatu et infra juxta nascendi tempora.
Herodes rex Christi nati verens infelix imperia,
Infremit totus, et erigit arma superba dextera,
Quaerit lucis et caeli regem cum mente turbida,
Ut extinguat qui vitam praestat per sua jacula.
Dum non valent intueri lucem splendidam nebulosa quaerentis pectora,
Ira fervet, fraudes auget Herodes saevus, ut perdat piorum agmina.
Castra militum dux iniquus aggregat;
Ferrum figit in membra tenera;
Inter ubera lac effundit,
Antequam sanguinis fierent coagula.
Hostis naturae natos eviscerat atque jugulat.
Ante prosternit, quam aetas parvula sumat robora.
Quam beata sunt Innocentum ab Herode caesa corpuscula.
Quam felices existunt matres, quae fuderunt talia pignora.
O dulces Innocentum acies ! O pia lactentium pro Christo certamina !
Parvulorum trucidantur millia, membris ex teneris manant lactis flumina.
Cives angelici veniunt in obviam,
Mira victoria vitae captat praemia turba candidissima.
Te, Christe, petimus mente devotissima,
Nostra qui venisti reformare saecula, Innocentum gloria
Perfrui nos concedas per aeterna.

Let the boys sound a high melody,

See, honouring the dances of the Innocents,

Whom the infant Christ today bore to the stars (heavens),

Whom, guilty of no offences, the madness of Herod's crime slaughtered

(by) Grinding (them) to pieces,

Throughout Bethlehem itself and through its borders,

Those newly born and up to the age of two years.

Every part of wretched King Herod dreading the authority of the Christ (now) born,

Roars out, and he raises his weapons with his proud right hand;

He seeks the King of Light and of the Sky with a frantic mind;

So that he who through his javelins might destroy him who grants life.

While the clouded heart of the searcher is not able to see the splendid light

His anger seethes; cruel Herod increases his crimes so that he may destroy the flock of the faithful.

The hostile general gathers the camp of soldiers;

He fixes his swords in tender limbs;

Milk runs between the breasts,

Before they are made thick with blood.

The enemy of nature disembowels and butchers the children.

He strikes down strength before the tiny generation should receive it.

How blessed are the small bodies of the Innocents slaughtered by Herod.

How fortunate appear the mothers who have poured out such relics.

O sweet army of Innocents! O pious combats of the Infants for Christ!

Thousands of tiny children were slaughtered with rivers of milk pouring from tender limbs.

Angelic citizens come into the meeting (fray);

With a wonderful victory the white robed host seizes the prizes of life.

We beg you with a very devout spirit, O Christ,

Who came to restore our age,

That you allow us to enjoy the glory of the Innocents

For all eternity.

Appendix C

Cantabant sancti canticum novum
ante sedem dei et agni
et resonabat terra in voces eorum.
Hi empti sunt ex hominibus primitiae Deo,
et Agno, et in ore eorum
non est inventum mendacium.
Et resonabat terra in voces eorum.

The Saints were singing a new song
before the throne of God and of the Lamb,
and earth resounded with their voices.
These children have been ransomed
from among men as the first offerings
to God and to the Lamb,
and in their mouths
no falsehood has been found.
And earth resounded with their voices.

Appendix D

Innocentes pro Christo infantes occisi sunt, ab iniquo rege lactentes interfecti sunt: ipsum sequuntur Agnum sine macula, et dicunt semper: Gloria tibi, Domine.

The innocent babes were slaughtered for Christ, the sucklings were put to death by the hostile king: they follow the spotless Lamb and continuously say: Glory be to you, O Lord.

Appendix E

At Matins, a double feast with two copes. The bidding *Mirabilem Deum* and the psalm *Venite* were sung as on the feast of St. Stephen with the hymn *Sanctorum meritis juncta*. The psalms were: *Beatus vir, Quare fremuerunt, Domine Deus in te speravi* with their corresponding antiphons *Novit Dominus, Rex terre, Deus iudex*. The first six readings from the sermon of St Severianus, which begins *Zelus qui tendat*, the three last from the homily of the Venerable (now Saint) Bede, which begin *De morte* before the gospel of St Matthew beginning *The angel appeared in dream to Joseph*. The responsories: *Sub altare, Effuderunt, Adoraverunt, Ex ore*. The psalm *In Domino confido*, antiphon *Mortis usum*, the psalm *Domine quis habitabit*, the responsories *Isti sunt sancti, Cantabant sancti, Isti sunt sancti*, antiphon *Quis ascendet*, psalm *Domini est terra*, antiphon *Innocentes*, psalm *Ad te levavi Domine*, antiphon *Filio regis*, psalm *Deus iudium*, responsory *Hii sunt qui cum mulieribus*, responsory (which was begun by two boys in silk copes, a line of which was sung in the group of boys in the middle of the choir) *Centum (The one hundred and forty-four thousand)*. After this the Boy Bishop censed and was censed by his chaplain in the manner of the adult bishop during solemnities.

At Lauds the usual psalms, with their respective antiphons *Herodes iratus, A bimatu et infra, Vox in Rama, Sub throno, Cantabant*, the chapter *Vidi supra montem*, the hymn *Rex gloriose*, the antiphon *O quam gloriosum est* which was given honour, the Boy Bishop beginning it three times on the order of his cantor according to the custom. The psalm *Benedictus*, the collect *Deus euius hodierna*, the commemorations of the Nativity, St Stephen and Saint John. At the end the Boy Bishop gave the blessing in the usual form.

At Terce, Sext and None, the first three antiphons from Lauds, the responses and versicles from the Common of Many Martyrs with the Alleluia were used.

After Terce there was a procession into the nave with the priest and other ministers of the altar dressed in sacred vestments as *Centum* was sung with the prose at the station together with a collect. Then the Boy Bishop gave the blessing in the manner of a true bishop at Mass. After a signal from the cantor he began the response *Descendit* (without a collect), which in short was said on the return of any procession into the choir up to the first Sunday after the octave of Epiphany.

At Mass the office *Ex ore* was intoned by the boys' cantor in the same way as an adult cantor. The collect used was for the commemoration of the Nativity, St Stephen and St John. The epistle was *Vidi supra montem*, as was sung on the preceding days; the gradual *Anima nostra* with the versicle *Laqueus* followed by the *Alleluia* and a further versicle *Sancti tui* were sung in the greater pulpit in the presence of the boys' cantor. These were followed by the sequence *Celsa pueri*, the antiphon *O quam gloriosum est regnum* and the gospel *Angelus Domini apparuit*. Then the creed was said after which the boys presented the offertory *Anima nostra*. Next came the secret *Sanctorum tuorum* (a Mass prayer), the secret of the Nativity, of Saint Stephen and Saint John. The communion was *Vox in Rama* and the post-communion *Voliva Domine* with the post-communion of the Nativity, of Saint Stephen and Saint John.

Appendix F

O quam gloriosum est regnum
In quo Christo gaudent omnes sancti!
Amicti stolis albis
Agnum sequuntur quocunque ierit.

Oh how glorious is the kingdom
In which all the saints rejoice in Christ!
Clothed in white apparel
They follow the Lamb wheresoever he may go.

Appendix G

Coutances

After Matins let all the boys gather in order to draw up their rota. The boys are allowed to assign the church dignitaries to the lesser offices. Let those ordained as deacons and subdeacons be assigned the thuribles and the larger and evidently the smaller candle-holders. They are able to assign to the true bishop, the cantor and the other canons the water, the towel, the missal, the fire and the bell as they please. However, let nothing unseemly or impertinent be assigned: the older men are assigned first and the younger last on the rota. Before Vespers of the priests are finished let all the boys gather behind the high altar and with them all the canons and the clerks who have not been admitted into sacred orders. And let their procession be organised with their Bishop dressed in amice, stole, tunicle, silk cope, with his mitre on his head, with gloves on his hands and with his ring and pastoral staff. And Vespers being finished, let the (Boy) Bishop begin the antiphon *O how glorious*. While singing this let the procession go out thus: the candle-bearers and thurifers go first; let those who are below holy orders follow; afterwards the rulers of the choir dressed in silk copes holding candles in their hands. Then (the) others two-by-two similarly holding candles; and let the cantor be vested in a silk cope; last of them let the Bishop proceed, preceded by the greater candlebearers, followed by two clergy of the second stall, called chaplains, vested in silk copes, with his chaplain and the vicar assigned to the cope in the rota, to be dressed in silk copes escorting him: let the chaplain be on his right and his deputy on the left. In this order let them leave through the great choir door and processing along the right hand side of the cathedral let them cross to the left hand side. And circling about let them return along the right hand side of the church to the centre of the nave where, a station having been made, the Bishop is censed by his two chaplains who kiss his hand. Afterwards let the thurifers cense the choir, one to the right and the other to the left. The antiphon finished, after the psalm, let the Bishop say the prayer with the opening, *The Lord be with you*. After the prayer, and *Let us bless the Lord*, let the two chaplains say *Humble yourselves* and let the choir respond *Thanks be to God.* When benediction has been given by the Bishop, let him begin the antiphon *The (virgin) mother not knowing (a man)* intoned to him by the cantor, with which let the procession go into the choir in the order in which it left. Let the Bishop go with his chaplain into the episcopal seat and let the cantor go to his stall; let the rulers of the choir go into the choir; let the two chaplains go into the higher stalls next to the bishop's seat. But let the deputy withdraw. And let the rest of the boys ascend to the higher stalls and let them be thus until Compline is finished. At the end of the antiphon let the two candle-bearers say the versicle and let the Bishop say the prayer preceded with *Let us pray.* Let two deacons begin the antiphon as a commemoration of St Stephen and let them say his versicle in the middle of the choir. Let the Bishop say the prayer and then *The Lord be with you.* Let the candle bearers say *Let us bless the Lord.* Let the Bishop begin Compline and say the chapter, and the peace(s) and the prayer. Let the two rulers of the choir together begin the prose and the antiphon on the *Nunc Dimittis.* Let the rulers of the choir intone the versicle to two of the senior members. And be it noted that whenever the Bishop says any prayer or chapter his chaplain should remove the mitre from his head until the said prayer or chapter is finished. Likewise be it noted that the canon responsible for the missal named in the rota, in his surplice, must bring the book of collects to the Bishop with a burning candle and hold it before him until he shall have finished the prayers; and likewise at the reading of the chapters and prayers at the following Matins and Vespers. The said canon, however, is able to do as he pleases with the candle after the Second Vespers. It is written in a later role that the canon having the prebends which are of Gaufridus de Argentonio which now is of Obertus de Vicecomitibus must perform this office because such is the honour of his prebend. After Compline let the Bishop remove his episcopal vestments and put on choir robes likewise as all the boys (in the choir). When this has been done let the Bishop go to his residence preceded by two candle-bearers in choir robes. Indeed, let the boys make an escort for him (themselves) singing *Greatly rejoicing* and do the same after Matins and the Mass.

At Matins, let the Bishop, dressed just as at Vespers, begin *O Lord (open) my lips* in his episcopal seat with his chaplain in silk cope accompanying him and with two chaplains standing in the higher stalls, just as at Compline in silk copes. Let four of the younger boys sing the invitatory, which, when concluded, a blessing having been asked of the Bishop, two having gone, let others direct the choir. Let one ruler of the choir begin the hymn and another the first antiphon. Let the rest be distributed just as at other double feasts and on Sundays. Let the cantor dressed in a silk cope intone all the psalms; let the verses after the nocturns be appointed to the canons or priests. After the end of the lessons let the readers come to the Bishop one at a time to beg for his blessing with bowed heads, and likewise those who sing the responsories. Let the three last readings be read in silk copes. Let one deacon or priest in a silk cope read the gospel as far as *And the remainder*. Let one boy continue with the homily. At the sixth or ninth responsory let all the boys having laid aside their black cloaks gather with their Bishop at the lectern. While the eighth responsory is (are) sung the Bishop goes to read the ninth lesson with his chaplain and with two other chaplains, preceded by the candle-bearers and thurifers, and as he goes past all must rise to their feet. When the Bishop has said, *Bless me, Lord*, let the chorus reply standing up: *Pray for us, father*. The lesson ended, he must incense the altars and relics with his deputy chaplain of the cope. The responsory and prose having finished, let the Bishop in the middle of the group begin the *Te Deum* and let it (the verses) be sung by the boys and the others alternately. Let all the boys sing the versicle after the hymn and return to their respective (proper) seats. Let Lauds be sung in the way designated by the antiphonaries. Let there be no procession, but the versicle being finished by the candle-bearers, let the Bishop begin the antiphon from the gospel begun for him by the cantor. That done, let him and the deputy chaplain, who is (holding) his cope, go to incense the altars and the Body of the Lord and the tombs of the bishops. After this let him (the Bishop) return to his throne; after he has been incensed by two chaplains let the vicar retire. The antiphon having been finished, let him say the collect, *The Lord be with you* having been said beforehand. Let a commemoration be made of the Nativity, one ruler of the choir beginning the antiphon, then the memorial of St Stephen, two deacons beginning the antiphon in the middle of the choir and saying his versicle, afterwards the memorial of St John by two priests in the aforementioned manner. Let the candle-bearers say *Let us bless the Lord*. After this let the blessing be (given) by the Bishop, as at First Vespers. Let the Bishop begin Prime in his episcopal seat and in unchanged choir robes. After the prayer has finished let the Bishop come down and all others in the lower stalls and let the lesson be read by one boy. Terce having been begun by the Bishop himself, let him go behind the altar and return to his throne vested in his episcopal robes to read the chapter and the prayer. If it be a Sunday, let there be a procession into the middle of the nave of the church just as on feasts (that are) semidoubles. Let the last Bishop proceed with his chaplains, the candle-bearers going first. Let the cantor go between the rulers of the choir. The responsory completed, let there be a memorial for the benefactors of the Church by the choir member appointed for the week or the priest who will celebrate, as on other Sundays. That done, let the blessing be (given) by the Bishop. Then let the procession return to the choir with the Bishop beginning the antiphon. Let the Bishop go to his seat and there say the prayer preceded by *Let us pray*. Let the two chaplains be in the higher stalls next to the seat of the Bishop. When the prayer is finished, let the priest, the deacon and the subdeacon go into the vestry to be vested in chasuble, dalmatic and tunicle, and meanwhile let the Mass be started by the rulers of the choir and the cantor. Let the Bishop go before the altar to the right of the priest to say the *I confess* and the absolution. That being done, let him return to his seat. Let the canon whose responsibility it is on that day to provide refreshments for the sacred ministers celebrate Mass. Let one deacon or priest read the gospel receiving the blessing from the Bishop and after the gospel let him incense and offer the open text to him to kiss it. And after the *Agnus Dei* let him give the kiss of peace to him. Let one subdeacon or deacon or priest sing the epistle with one boy dressed in a silk cope. Let it be noted that the Bishop must bless the incense just as is made clear in double feasts. One of the boys is allowed to be an acolyte if he has been promoted to that order, or, if it pleases the boys, let one subdeacon perform that office, or a deacon or a priest. Three boys sing the *Gradale*. All the boys dressed in silk copes sing the *Alleluia* with their Bishop. Then let them begin the prose and let it (the verses) be sung by them and by others alternately. When it is finished let then return to their places; let the creed be said (and) the preface *Because through (the mystery) of the incarnation* and the (Christmas) *communicantes*. The Offertory having been begun, let the priest taking the chalice in his hands turn to the Bishop so that the Bishop may bless the chalice. Then let all the boys and others to whom it might be pleasing make an offering to him, kissing his hand. After this, if he wishes, let him wash his hands. When Mass has ended with *Go, it is ended* let the Bishop give the blessing. Afterwards let him begin Sext; then let him return behind the altar to take off his episcopal vestments and, his choir robes having been put on, let him return to his seat to say the chapter and prayer. On this day let the ministers use the red vestments. Let the Bishop dressed in choir robes begin Nones at his throne and then let him go behind the altar and, dressed in his episcopal robes, let him return to his throne to say the chapter and the prayer.

At Vespers let the rulers of the choir begin the antiphon *With you is the principality* and let the other antiphons be begun by the boys in pairs at the eagle. Let the Bishop read the chapter. Let the responsory *O How glorious* be sung by all the boys in the higher pulpitum having laid aside their black cloaks. Let the prose

Greatly rejoicing be started by the boys in the same place and (the verses) sung alternately by these boys and the others of low degree. Let the versicle *Let us rejoice* be said by the boys in the same place. Before the prose is finished, let the Bishop go to his throne to begin the antiphon of the gospel. Then let him and the aforementioned deputy go to cense just as at Matins. The prayer ended with *Let us bless the Lord*, let the Bishop give the blessing, When that has been done, let him say *Deposuit* and at once let the chosen Bishop, with the pastoral staff having been handed to him by the boys, go before the altar and after the altar has been kissed let him be escorted (carried) to his residence by the same boys. And meanwhile, with the commotion being ended, let there be a procession to the altar of St Thomas the Martyr through the great door of the choir with this antiphon: *Hic est vere vir*. There follows the *Magnificat* psalm. And meanwhile let the altar be censed by the canon who celebrated the Mass that day and by the deputy of the cope. When the antiphon is finished with a *neuma*, let him say the prayer introduced by *Let us pray*, and after the prayer let there be said *Let us bless the Lord* by the rulers of the choir who ought to be of the second stall. As the procession returns let one ruler of the choir begin the antiphon of the memorial of the Nativity and let the procession return through the left door of the choir. Let the two candle-bearers say the versicle. Then let there be the memorials of St Stephen and St John as ordered for Matins. At the end of Compline the antiphon *Miserere* is begun by the principal ruler of the choir and let Compline be said according the order set out for semidouble feasts.

Appendix H

Toul

In the church of Toul, so to speak, the two Bishops of the Innocents were elected: one from his order by the canons, who was held to supply the expenses of the feast under pain of disgrace and the witholding of his canon's benefits; the other, of the boys or junior clergy to take on the role of the Bishop.

Concerning the feast and Bishop of the Innocents...

In any year that feast is assigned to one canon following the order of his appointment to his prebend, and the appointment itself is made after supper on the day of Holy Innocents. For, he who has completed the feast gives thanks to the Bishop and to all his companions and asks to be forgiven if he has failed in anything, and finally he gives a cap of rosemary or selection of other flowers to the Bishop himself so that he might hand it over to the canon who is next on the rota to make the feast next year, or to his deputy: for if he be absent he will have to be asked by letter from the chapter for three months before the day to send a proxy to it. Then if he shall have come or have sent his deputy to receive and undertake this burden he is admitted; and if there is doubt about poor behaviour or mockery it is examined carefully. And if indeed he having been admonished withdrew from the prebend, he who might be succeeding should not be accepted thereto until warned that he would be celebrating this feast on behalf and in the name of his predecessor and not in his own (name). If, however, he scorn to provide for the coming feast a black cassock is suspended on a pole in the middle of the choir and stays there as an object of mockery so long as it pleases the subdeacons and the boys of the choir. And in this these things they are not obliged to obey the chapter.

The same would be done against the existing prebendary, if he similarly scorned, not giving up prebend, whether absent or present, nor will he ever be able partake in whatsoever emoluments of the church, until he makes this feast of this kind and puts right his aforesaid contempt. But strictly speaking he who gives the feast itself is not held to give a party except to those counted as Innocents. There are made there moralities or miracle plays with farses and similar entertainments, always moral, however.

And it is not to be neglected that on the first Saturday in Advent all the boys and ferial subdeacons, who are counted in the number of the said Innocents gather after Compline and there they choose one Bishop from the boys for the present Feast of Innocents, who immediately is taken up and, as all sing the *Te Deum*, and certainly with the bells ringing, is carried to the throne behind the altar of The Blessed Virgin where the Bishops of Toul are first enthroned, and there he sits. And at the end of the *Te Deum* the other one of them says the collect of the feast of the Holy Innocents and then the Bishop assumes his office, so that with the coming feast, vested in mitre and pontifical insignia, with his pastoral staff carried before him, he performs the office of the Bishop at each Vespers of the eve and of the day and at Matins and Mass sitting or standing just as he pleases in the higher stall of the Bishop and he gives the blessing and the Lord Bishop gives way to the same (boy) for the said Hours.

Appendix I

Padua

The vigil of the Innocents. At Vespers as above. At the *Magnificat* the antiphon *Iste est discipulus*. And then the priests put off their copes and two acolytes put on the copes and then take candles and books to the scholars. The collect of St John finished, one of the aforementioned acolytes takes the antiphon of the Innocents to the senior acolyte and the Bishop sings the verse and the collect of the Innocents and afterwards there follow the antiphons, versicles and collects of the Nativity and St Stephen. And thus Vespers is sung when there is no Boy Bishop. But when there is a Boy Bishop then, when the collect of St John is finished, the Boy Bishop goes out from the lower sacristy, prepared with his clerks and chaplains in copes, with cross, thurible and candles preceding, and they go in procession to the altar of St Daniel singing *Centum.* And then the Boy Bishop ascends to the altar with candles preceding and censes it, and the acolyte receiving the thurible censes the Boy Bishop, the acolytes who rule the choir, and then the canons and others clerics and scholars according to the order noted above. The responsory being finished, one of the acolytes begins the antiphon for the *Magnificat*, namely *Istorum est enim regnum celorum.* The collect *Deus cuius hodierna die.* And there follow the antiphons and collects of the Nativity and St Stephen, as mentioned above, and the Boy Bishop says the collects. And afterwards three acolytes or other clerics sing and follow with *Benedicamus Domino* and the Boy Bishop blesses the priest and the people.

At Matins the Boy Bishop begins Matins. If the Boy Bishop is not there, then the weekly priest without a cope begins. Four acolytes in copes sing the bidding in the middle of the choir, because the Boy Bishop puts his seat next to the *pergamum* and while the bidding is being sung, the Boy Bishop goes and censes the altar and all are censed according to the above order. And then two acolytes in copes lead the choir and offer the antiphons first to the Bishop, then to the scholars beginning with the younger ones, and thus there follows the proper reading namely *Sub altare Dei* with the bidding and antiphons and psalms of the martyrs. The Boy Bishop both says and does everything that a bishop would do and say. Six lessons are read from the proper lectionary, namely *Hodie fratres carissimi, natalem illorum infantium,* etc. The senior acolyte reads the first lesson and so by downward degrees the acolytes read the lessons. The deacon reads the homily, namely *Angelus Domini apperuit.* The Boy Bishop reads the ninth lesson. The *Te Deum* is not sung, but when the ninth lesson is finished the Boy Bishop goes with the priest behind the high altar singing the ninth responsory, namely *Centum…*; and then Lauds is sung with the proper antiphons, namely *Herodes iratus est.* And in this way the psalms follow, because from one side they begin *Dominus regnavit*; from the other side the second verse; those who remain in the choir on one side say the third verse; on the other they say the fourth; and in this order follow all the psalms of Lauds and *Benedictus Dominus Deus Israel.* Chapter *Vidi supra montem.* Verse *Hii sunt qui cum mulieribus.* Antiphon at *Benedictus, A bimatu et infra.* Collect *Deus cuius hodierna die.* And there follow the antiphons and collects of the Nativity of the Lord, St Stephen and St John.

Matins being finished, the Boy Bishop blesses the priest and the people. But if there is no Boy Bishop, Matins and Lauds are sung in the choir, not behind the altar.

At Mass. After Prime, a priest says the Mass of the Boy Bishop at the altar of the Holy Cross, and there on the right side of the altar the Boy Bishop is prepared in his cope and mitre and with his chaplains. The Office is *Out of the mouths of babes…* The epistle *Vidi supra montem Syon*

The reader dressed in a plain straight garment reads this and holds in his hand a wooden spoon which he throws towards the people. And there are some men who follow the aforementioned spoon and go around the church seeking the infant with his mother, namely Christ with the Blessed Virgin Mary. And there is someone dressed like a woman who sits on a donkey, having her son on her lap; and one who represents Joseph leads the donkey, fleeing through the church, signifying the Virgin fleeing with the boy into Egypt according to what the angel of the Lord had said to Joseph in a dream.

The *Gloria* and *Alleluia* are not said, but in place of the *Alleluia, Laus tibi, Christe* is said. The gospel *Angelus Domini apperuit* which the deacon says only with a stole. After the gospel, the Boy Bishop dressed in cope and mitre, with his staff, comes down with his chaplains and priests to the steps before the altar of the Holy Cross and sitting there he takes the offering from the people, which is his own offering. When the offering has been received, one of his chaplains makes his confession as seems good; and afterwards the Boy Bishop blesses the priest and people with his blessings.

Mass being over, another Mass begins for the boys in plainsong with the same offertory, collect, epistle and gospel as at the first Mass. The gospel being finished, the women offer money and candles for the dead boys; and afterwards Mass is finished.

At Terce, Sext and Nones, the first three antiphons of Lauds before the psalms. The chapter at Terce *Vidi*; the Chapter at Sext *Et audivi vocem*; the Chapter at Nones *Et vocem quam audivi*. The responsory for the martyrs, which the senior acolyte says and he begins the antiphon before the psalms.

At Vespers, everything on the eve of St Thomas the Martyr as above. Chapter *Vidi supra montem*; for the *Magnificat* the antiphon *Innocentes pro Christo*; collect as above. Collect of St Thomas *Deus pro cuius ecclesia*. Afterwards there follow the antiphons and collects of the Nativity, St Stephen and St John. Compline as above.

Appendix J

Vespers of the same day having been sung, the Bishop himself with mimes and pipes proceeds through the city with his entourage through the roads along which the general processions are made... On the octave of the Holy Innocents again the Bishop in his robes goes with all his entourage to the church of St Genevieve where the anthem having been sung for the Virgin with the collect he goes to the parish house of that church or elsewhere, where the master and brothers of the house of God with which the same church has been joined, shall have provided the cake, apples, nuts, etc., suitable for refreshments; and there the officers are established for fines concerning the defects and excesses committed in the Divine Office during the whole year. These fines are applied for the feasting of the Bishop and the others numbered among the Innocents on the day after Holy Innocents when all go through the city after lunch with hidden appearances in different clothes, and if any farses are to take place, but at a dry time, let everything (everyone) be in some places of the city with all (moral) integrity, and in returning, they go a second time to the canon or his deputy and the place, where was made the feast of the Innocents , who is bound still to merit to serve refreshments out of the left-overs of the previous day.

Appendix K

The Prose of the Ass

Orientis partibus,
Adventavit asinus,
Pulcher et fortissimus,
Sarcinis aptissimus.
    Hez, sir Asne, Hez!

Hic in collibus Sichen
Iam nutritus sub Ruben,
Transiit per Jordanem
Saliit in Bethlehem
    Hez, sir Asne, Hez!

Saltu vincit hinnulos,
Dagmas et capreolos,
Super dromedarios
Velox Madianeos.
    Hez, sir Asne, Hez!

Aurum de Arabia,
Thus et myrram de Sabba
Tulit in ecclesia
Virtus asinaria
    Hez, sir Asne, Hez!

Dum trahit vehicula,
Multa cum sarcinula,
Illius mandibula
Dura terit pabula.
　　Hez, sir Asne, Hez!

Cum aristis ordeum
Comedit et carduum;
Triticum a palae
Segregat in area.
　　Hez, sir Asne, Hez!

Amen dicas, asine,
Iam satur ex gramine,
Amen, amen itera,
Aspernare vetera.
　　Hez, sir Asne, Hez!

Notes

Introduction

[1] J Gregory, *Episcopus Puerorum in Die Innocentium,* Opera Posthuma, London, 1649.

[2] J R Planché, 'On the Sepulchral Effigies in Salisbury Cathedral', *Journal of the British Archaeological Society*, vol 15, 1854, pp. 121-124.

[3] E Hautcoeur, *Histoire de l'église collégiale et du chapitre de Saint-Pierre de Lille*, 1897, p. 224.

Chapter 1

[1] Some of the more common alternative names for the Boy Bishop include: *Episcopus Puerorum, Episcopus Iuvenum, Episcopus Nicholatensis, Episcopus Innocentum, Parvulus, Praesul, Episcopus Puerilis, Episcopus Sancti Nicolai, Episcopus Elemosinarie, Schul-Bischof, Apfeln-Bischof, Bisbeto, Obispillo,* Child Bishop, St Nicholas Bishop, The Boys' Bishop, Bishop of the Little Ones, Barn (Bairn) Bishop, Bishop Nicholas, Bishop of the Almonry, Bishop of the Choristers.

[2] H Denfile, *Auctarium Chartularii Universitatis Parisiensis*, vol III, pp. 166-175.

[3] D H Robertson, *Sarum Close*, London, 1938.

[4] G H Pertz, *Monumenta Germaniae Historica Scriptorum*, vol XXIII, Hanover, 1874, pp. 144-145.

[5] E Martene, *De Antiquis Ecclesiae Ritibus*, vol III (Liber IV Caput XIII), p. 40.

[6] J Huizinga, *The Waning of the Middle Ages*, reprinted Penguin, 1987.

Chapter 2

[1] I Mortimer, *The Time Traveller's Guide to Medieval England*, The Bodley Head, London, 2008.

[2] J M Clark, *The Abbey of St Gall as a Centre of Literature and Art*, Cambridge, 1926, pp. 216-217.

[3] J M J Fletcher, *The Boy Bishop at Salisbury and Elsewhere*, Salisbury, 1921, p. 5.

[4] C E Pearsall (ed), *The History and Genealogy of the Pearsall Family in England and America,* San Francisco, 1928, p. 107.

[5] Beletus, *de Divin. Offic.,* cap 72 and cap 120.

[6] C H Evelyn-White, 'The Boy Bishop (Episcopus Puerorum) of Mediaeval England Pt 1', *Journal of the British Archaeological Association,* vol XL, 1905, p. 36.

[7] C H Timperely, *A Dictionary of Printers and Printing*, London , 1839, p. 116.

[8] A Chérest, 'Nouvelles Recherches sur la Fête des Innocents et la Fête des Fous', *Bulletin de la Société des Sciences de L'Yonne,* vol 7, 1853, p. 9.

[9] Lucian, *Saturnalia*

[10] Calendar of Coroner's Rolls for the City of London A.D. 1300-1378, 1913, p. 25.

[11] B A Hanawalt, *Growing Up in Medieval London,* OUP, Oxford, 1993, p. 64.

[12] P Ariès, *Centuries of Childhood*, Paris, 1960. (English version Jonathan Cape, 1962.)

[13] N D Shergold, *A History of the Spanish Stage*, Oxford, 1967, p. 23.

Chapter 3

[1] For example, see T Warton, Hazlitt (ed), *The History of English Poetry*, vol II, 1871, pp. 230-232.

[2] E F Rimbault, 'Two Sermons Preached by the Boy Bishop', *The Camden Miscellany,* vol VII, 1875, p. xxiii.

[3] A F Leach, 'The Schoolboys' Feast', *The Fortnightly Review*, vol 14, 1896, p. 132.

[4] J E Millard, *Historical Notices of the Office of Choristers*, 1848, p. 50.

[5] E K Chambers, *The Medieval Stage*, OUP, London, 1903, p. 360.

[6] C D Du Cange, *Glossarium mediae et infimae Latinitatis conditum a Du Cangio, auctum a monachis Ordinis S. Benedicit, cum supplementis Carpenterii suisque digessit* G A L Henschel. Editio nova, aucta a L Favre, 10 vols, 1883-7, s. v. *Kalendae*.

[7] Johannes Boemus, *Omnium Gentium Mores, Leges et Ritus*, Antwerp, 1562.

[8] D H Robertson.

[9] *Registr. Archiv. Eccles. Ebor.* MSS.

[10] M J Rigollot, *Monnaies inconnues des Evêques des Innocens, des Fous, et quelque autres Associations singulières du meme Temps*, 1837, p. 50.

[11] ibid., p. 50.

Chapter 4

[1] In 1263.

[2] W Sparrow Simpson (ed), *Registrum Statutorum et Consuetudinum Ecclesiae Cathedralis Sancti Pauli Londiniensis*, London, 1873, p. 92.

[3] C Wordsworth (ed), *Ceremonies and Processions of the Cathedral Church of Salisbury*, Cambridge, 1901, p. 52.

[4] Matt. 20:16. (Biblical references following Vulgate/Douai system.)

[5] Matt. 18: 3-5.

[6] Magnificat.

[7] *Symond's Lesson for All Manner of Children* (15th century poem).

[8] C Wordsworth, pp. 52-58.

[9] Apocalypse 14:4-5.

[10] The cathedral canon in charge of liturgy and music.

[11] Wisdom 5:16.

[12] Psalm 149:5 (Psalm numbers using Greek/Catholic numbering).

[13] Psalm 116.

[14] See Appendix A.

[15] Psalm 67:36.

[16] Luke 1:68-80.

[17] Commemorations of the Nativity, St Stephen and St John.

[18] In fact, a *Deposuit* could occur in two places: during the *Magnificat* at Vespers (usually on the Eve of Holy Innocents) when the Boy Bishop took the bishop's throne; and during the *Magnificat* at Vespers (usually on the feast of Holy Innocents) when the Boy Bishop relinquished the throne.

[19] A commemoration of a feast on the eighth day, given to the most important feasts.

[20] Bishop Grandisson's *Ordinale*.

[21] 'Missale ad Usum Insignis Ecclesiae Eboracensis', *The Surtees Society*, vol 1, Durham, 1874, pp. 23-25.

[22] Chambers translates as "rushes". However, he does make an uncharacteristic error in attributing the statute to Lincoln and not to York. E K Chambers, p. 356.

[23] *The Statute Book* (York) YM M1/1/b.

[24] Psalm 8:3.

[25] Note that the word "choir" has two meanings (a) a group of singers (b) the part of a church around the high altar where the services would be sung.

[26] The prayer for the day.

[27] See Appendix B.

[28] W Sparrow Simpson , p. 91.

[29] Quoted in W Andrews, *Curious Church Customs*, London, 1898, p. 3.

[30] Hereford Breviary.

[31] C D Du Cange, s. v. *Kalendae*.
  A Gasté, *Les Drames Liturgiques de la Cathédrale de Rouen*, Evreux, 1893, pp. 35-36.

[32] The song of the Blessed Virgin when she learns that she is to bear the Son of God. Luke 1:46-55.

[33] A Gasté, pp. 36-37.

[34] A Picard, *Ordinaire et coutumier de l'Eglise Cathédrale de Bayuex*, Paris, 1902, pp. 69-72.

[35] See Appendix C.

[36] See Appendix D.

[37] For a full description see Appendix E.

[38] Martin Dudley sees a slight problem here. He believes that there is a confusion in the rubrics, because the pastoral staff has already been handed over. But it might equally have been the case that the first offering of the staff merely constituted the "election" and the staff would then be returned to the outgoing Boy Bishop who would then go to the altar where the new boy would be vested. M R Dudley, 'Natalis Innocentum', *The Church and Childhood*, D Wood (ed), Oxford, 1994, p. 238.

[39] A Gasté, pp. 39-43.

[40] See Appendix F.

[41] Those carrying the burning incense in metal vessels swung on chains.

[42] Someone who led the singing.

[43] For full details see Appendix G.

[44] C D Du Cange, s. v. *Kalendae*.

[45] See Appendix H for a full account.

[46] J Gregory, *Episcopus Puerorum In Die Innocentium*, 1671.

[47] P N Grenier, *Introduction à l'Histoire général de la Province de Picardie*, 1856, p. 355.

[48] F A Specht, *Geschichte des Unterrichtswens in Deutschland*, 1967 (reprinted), pp. 216-229.

[49] J M Clark, pp. 215-217.

[50] F A Dürr, 'Commentatio Historica de Episcopo Puerorum', *Thesaurus Iuris Ecclesiastica*, vol III, J Schmidt, 1772, pp. 58-83.

[51] Bibl. Capit., Padua, MS S Ordin. Patavinense saec. xiii, fol 50^v- 53^v.

[52] It was usual for clerics to play the parts in such dramas.

[53] See Appendix I for a full account.

[54] R B Donovan, *The Liturgical Drama in Medieval Spain*, Toronto, 1958, p. 190.

[55] N D Shergold, p. 22.

[56] ibid., p. 9.

[57] R B Donovan, pp. 195- 196.

[58] J S Arjona, *El teatro en Sevilla en los siglos*, Madrid, 1887, pp. 16-24.

[59] A Gasté, pp. 44-45.

[60] E F Rimbault, pp. xxvi-xxviii.

M J Rigollot.

Chapter 5

[1] Rock D, *The Church of Our Fathers*. vol III, part 2, London, 1852. p. 216.

[2] W Sparrow Simpson (ed), *Registrum Statutorum et Consuetudinum Ecclesiae Cathedralis Sancti Pauli Londiniensis*, London, 1873, pars septima, cap 6, p. 129.

[3] ibid., pp. 92-93.

[4] E F Rimbault, pp. xi-xvi and Appendix.

[5] As the cathedral at York is usually called.

[6] I Mortimer, p. 100.

[7] Y Dahhaoui, 'Voyages d'un prélat festif', *Revue historique* 3/2006 (N°639), pp. 677-694.

[8] Those who undertook the cathedral canons' duties in their absence.

[9] 33p in present currency. In old currency 12d (pence) = 1s (shilling); 20s = £1.

[10] T Warton, The History of English Poetry, vol III, London, 1840, p. 251.

[11] Quoted in a modern Service Booklet for the Boy Bishop.

[12] C D Du Cange, s. v. *Kalendae*.

[13] See appendix J.

[14] C M Gayley, *Plays of our Forefathers*, London, 1908, pp. 60-61.

[15] Paris, BnF, ms. lat. 17123, p 357, quoted in Y Dahhaoui, pp. 677-694.

[16] M J Rigollot, pp. 21-24.

[17] P N Grenier, p. 355ff.

[18] F A Specht, pp. 225-227.

[19] F A Dürr, pp. 58-83.

[20] K Young, *The Drama of the Medieval Church*, vol 2, Oxford, 1933, pp. 106-109.

[21] *Statutes* of Bishop Grandisson (1337) quoted in T Warton, *The History of English Poetry*, London, 1840, vol II, p. 30.

[22] E F Rimbault, pp. xviii-xix.

[23] M J Fletcher, *The Boy Bishop at Salisbury and Elsewhere*, Salisbury, 1921, pp. 18-19, quoting Nicholls and Taylor, *Bristol Past and Present*, vol II, p. 162.

[24] T Warton, *The History of English Poetry*, London, 1840, vol III, p. 267.

[25] T Percy (ed), *The Regulations and Establishment of the Household of Algernon Percy the fifth Earl of Northumberland*, 1827, p. 343.

[26] ibid., p. 340.

[27] M J Rigollot, pp. 25-26.

[28] ibid., pp 13-14.

[29] ibid., p. 13.

[30] ibid., p. 34.

[31] ibid., p. 27.

[32] A F Leach, 'The Schoolboys' Feast', *The Fortnightly Review*, vol 14, 1896, p. 135.

[33] M J Rigollot, p. 32.

[34] ibid., pp. 40-41.

[35] M Poinsignon, *Histoire Générale de la Champagne et de la Brie*, vol II, 2nd ed., Chalons-sur-Marne, 1897, pp. 29-30.

[36] A Chérest, pp. 7-82.

[37] E K Chambers, p. 347.

E Martene, *De Antiquis Ecclesiae Ritibus Libris Tres*, vol III, Venice, 1783, p. 38.

Chapter 6

[1] Of these, two are to be found in E F Rimbault. The other is by Erasmus in two versions, Latin, *Concio de Puero Jesu*, Ghent, 1513? and English, J H Lupton (ed), *Sermon on the Chylde Jesus*, London, 1901.

[2] *On Civility in Children.*

[3] E F Rimbault, p. xxxvi.

[4] Matt 18:3.

[5] Since the sermons were written in the English of the period, in quoting them I have changed the spelling slightly and sometimes altered the English a little to make them easier to understand.

[6] John 3:1-15.

[7] Matt 11:12.

[8] Genesis 4. Cain, the first murderer, slew his innocent brother, Abel.

[9] The prophet Jeremias or Jeremiah.

[10] B A Hanawalt.

[11] A Martindale, 'The Child in the Picture: a Medieval Perspective', D Wood (ed) *The Church and Childhood*, Oxford, 1994.

[12] mary/marry = indeed.

[13] cure = place of care, analogous to a priest having the cure of souls.

[14] A Latin grammarian whose work provided the basis for Latin teaching in many schools.

[15] 1 Corinthians 13:11.

[16] Simony is the serious sin of paying for the sacraments or for positions in the Church.

[17] Statutes quoted in W Sparrow Simpson, p. 92.

[18] The great Roman orator, Cicero.

[19] John 1:9.

[20] Matt 28:18.

[21] It runs to about 42 pages.

[22] J M J Fletcher, p. 18, quoting Nicholls and Taylor, p. 162.

[23] R B Donovan, p. 65.

Chapter 7

[1] Jones and Dayman, *Sarum Statutes*, p. 75.

[2] O Bled, 'La Fête des Innocents dans l'église collégiale de Saint-Omer', extract from *Bulletin historique* de la Société des Antiquaires de la Morinie, Saint Omer, 1887, quoted in E Hautcoeur, *Histoire de l'église collégiale et du chapitre de Saint-Pierre de Lille*, vol 2, Paris, 1896-1897, p. 225.

[3] E Hautcoeur, pp. 225-226.

[4] C Hidé, *Bulletin de la Societé Academique de Laon*, vol 13, pp. 123-124.

[5] E Fleury, *Cinquante Ans de l'Histoire du Chapitre de N-D de Laon*, Laon, 1875, pp. 52-53.

[6] See Chapter 5.

[7] M Beziers, *Histoire de Sommaire de la Ville de Bayeux*, Caen, 1773, p. 60.

[8] A Gasté, p. 37.

[9] A Chérest, pp. 62-63.

[10] H F Feilberg, *Jul*, Copenhagen, 1904, p. 254, quoted in C A Miles, *Christmas Ritual and Tradition,* vol 2, 1912.

[11] L Petit de Julleville, *Histoire du théâtre en France*, Paris, 1886, pp. 37-38.

[12] C D Du Cange, s. v. *Kalendae*.

[13] T Warton, *The History of English Poetry*, London, 1840, vol III, p. 266.
    E F Rimbault, p. xx.

[14] P N Grenier, p. 359.

[15] *O miserum saeculum!... solo gestu externoque habitu spectabiles sola barba et pallio philosophi, caetera pecudes* – quoted in P N Grenier, pp. 358-359.

[16] A F Leach, p. 137.

[17] Quoted in A F Leach, p. 137.

[18] An inventory of the documents of Chartres Cathedral reveals between 1724 and 1726 *Permission aux enfants de choeur de célébrer l'octave des Saintes-Innocents.*

[19] E Fleury, pp. 53-54.

[20] F A Specht, pp. 227-228.

[21] F A Dürr, pp. 58-83.

[22] E K Chambers, pp. 351-352.

[23] Quoted in A F Schack, *Historia de la literature y del arte dramática en España*, Madrid, 1885, vol I, pp. 247-248.

[24] One of the sacraments of the Church.

[25] N D Shergold, p. 8.

[26] J S Arjona, pp. 21-24.

[27] J P W Crawford, 'A Note on the Boy Bishop in Spain', *Romanic Review*, vol 12, 1921, p. 148.

[28] H F Feilberg.

[29] C M Gayley, p. 68.

[30] E K Chambers, p. 361.

[31] C D Du Cange, s. v. *Kalendae*.

[32] A Gasté, pp. 44-45.

[33] E K Chambers, p. 360.

[34] H E Reynolds (ed), *Wells Cathedral: Its Foundation, Constitutional History, and Statutes*, Leeds, pp. 75, 87-88.

[35] F C Hingeston-Randolph, *The Register of John de Grandisson, Bishop of Exeter*, Part III, London, 1899, pp. 1213-1215.

[36] Wilkins's *Concilia*, quoted in E F Rimbault, pp. xx-xxi.

[37] J G Nicholls (ed), *The Diary of Henry Machyn from 1550 AD to 1563 AD*, London, 1848, 13th November, 5th December, 1554.

[38] Cattley (ed), *The Acts and Monuments of John Foxe*, vol VIII, London, 1839, pp. 726-727.

[39] J G Nicholls.

[40] T Warton, *The History of English Poetry*, London, 1840, vol III, p. 265.

[41] Quoted in D Morse-Boycott, *The Boy Bishop Book*, 1946, p. 16. This book seems to have been privately printed and distributed but is available in the British Library, shelfmark 3478.bb.59. I can find no other source for this account.

[42] C H Evelyn-White, 'The Boy Bishop (Episcopus Puerorum) of Mediaeval England Pt 1', pp. 40-41.

Chapter 8

[1] E K Chambers, gives a very comprehensive account, pp. 274-335.
   See also C D Du Cange, s. v. *Kalendae*
         L Petit de Julleville, pp. 29-41
         C M Gayley, pp. 47-50
         A Chérest, pp. 7-82.

[2] Quoted in E K Chambers, p 294, note (2).

[3] M Harris, 'A Rough and Holy Liturgy: A Reassessment of the Feast of Fools'. Katja Gvozdeva and Werner Röcke (ed), *Risus Sacer – Risus Risible: Interaktionsfelder von Sakralität und Gelächter im kulturellen und historischen Wandel*, Peter Lang, Bern, 2009.
   J Taylor, 'Prophetic "Play" and Symbolist Plot in the Beauvais *Daniel*', C Davidson, C J Gianakaris and J H Stroupe, (eds), *The Drama of the Middle Ages: Comparative and Critical Essays*, AMS Press, New York, 1982, p. 32.

[4] C D Du Cange, s. v. *Kalendae*.

[5] H Villetard (ed), *Office de Pierre de Corbeil (Office de la Circoncision) improprement appelé "Office des Fous"*, Paris: Alphonse Picard, 1907.

[6] See Appendix K. It differed slightly at Beauvais.

[7] P N Grenier, pp. 363-364.

[8] A garment similar to a surplice but with tighter sleeves.

[9] A Chérest, pp. 65-67.
[10] J S Arjona, pp. 1-16.

Chapter 9

[1] 1946. This seems to have been privately printed and distributed but is available in the British Library, shelfmark 3478.bb.59.
[2] Morse-Boycott used the term *"sealing"* rather than *"consecration"* to avoid giving any impression that the boy was in holy orders.
[3] For which I have no publishing details.
[4] Appropriately enough for a choir school, the patron saint of music.

Chapter 10

[1] These are taken form a variety of sources:
Archaeologia, vol LII, p. 221ff.
J M J Fletcher, p. 10.
C H Evelyn-White, 'The Boy Bishop (Episcopus Puerorum) of Mediaeval England Pt 2', *Journal of the British Archaelogical Association*, vol XL, 1905, pp. 240-243.
C Wordsworth.
E K Chambers, pp. 336-371.
W Andrews, p. 3.
A F Leach, pp. 132-133.
'Durham Account Rolls', *The Surtees Society*, vols I-III.
W Boys, *A History of Sandwich in Kent*, 1892.
W Sparrow Simpson p. 92.
J Raine, 'Fabric Rolls of York Minster', *The Surtees Society*, vol XXV, 1859, p. 214.
A Gasté, pp. 35-36.
[2] E Duffy, *The Voices of Morebath*, Yale University Press, New Haven and London, 2001.
[3] J Stuart (ed), *Extracts from the Council Register of the Burgh of Aberdeen*, vol I, p. 186.
[4] C H Evelyn-White, 'The Boy Bishop (Episcopus Puerorum) of Mediaeval England Pt 2', p. 251.
[5] Bibl. Capit., MS 77, Consueta Barcinonensis seac. xiv-xv, fol.364, R B Donovan, "The Liturgical Drama in Medieval Spain", Toronto, 1958, p 191.
[6] M J Rigollot, pp. 47-48.
[7] E K Chambers, p. 349 (note 14).
[8] E K Chambers, p. 349, note [8].
[9] F A Gasquet, *The Old English Bible and Other Essays*, London, 1897, p. 251.
[10] E K Chambers, p. 365.
[11] T Warton, *The History of English Poetry*, Hazlitt (ed), London, vol II, 1871, p. 230.
[12] C Wordsworth, p. 52.
[13] Du Tilliot, *Memoires pour Servir a l'Histoire de la Fête des Foux*, Lausanne, 1751.
[14] J M J Fletcher, p. 14.
[15] R B Donovan, p. 191.

[16] ibid., p. 191.

[17] J J A Pilot de Thorey, *Usages, Fêtes, et Coutumes existent ou ayant existé en Dauphiné*, vol 1, Grenoble, 1884, p. 181.

[18] E K Chambers, p. 351.

[19] E F Rimbault, p. xvii.

[20] T Dickson (ed), *Accounts of the Lord High Treasurer of Scotland*, vol 1, p. ccxlvi.

[21] N D Shergold, p. 23.

[22] D Lysons, *The Environs of London*, vol 1, London, 1792, p. 310.

[23] C H Evelyn-White, 'The Boy Bishop (Episcopus Puerorum) of Mediaeval England Pt 2', p. 239.

[24] H N Hillebrand, *The Child Actors*, New York, 1964, p. 76.

[25] Louth Churchwardens' Accounts, quoted in E Howlett, 'Boy Bishops', *Curious Church Gleanings*, W Andrews (ed), Hull, 1896, p. 247.

[26] *Ordo IX Lugdunensis*.

[27] N D Shergold, pp. 21-22.

[28] E K Chambers, p. 319.

[29] F A Dürr, pp. 58-83

[30] E K Chambers, p. 359.

[31] J M J Fletcher, p. 10.

[32] ibid., p. 10.

[33] C H Evelyn-White, 'The Boy Bishop (Episcopus Puerorum) of Mediaeval England Pt 2', p. 238.

[34] *Archaeologia*, vol XXVI, p. 342.

[35] R B Donovan, p. 65.

[36] ibid., p. 191.

[37] A Tille, *Die Geschichte der deutschen Weihnacht*, Leipsic, 1893, p. 31.

[38] P N Grenier, p. 359.

[39] T Warton, *The History of English Poetry*, Hazlitt (ed), London, vol II, 1871, p 231

[40] W Dugdale, *Monasticon Anglicanum*, vol III, London, 1846, p. 360.

[41] R B Donovan, p. 65.

[42] ibid., p. 191.

[43] E K Chambers, p. 349.

[44] T Boutiot, *Histoire de la Ville de Troyes*, Troyes, vol III, 1873, p. 20.

[45] N D Shergold, p. 23.

[46] R B Donovan, p. 192.

[47] H E Reynolds, pp. 75, 87-88.

[48] J M J Fletcher, p. 10.

[49] R B Donovan, p. 192.

[50] C H Evelyn-White, 'The Boy Bishop (Episcopus Puerorum) of Mediaeval England Pt 1', p. 37.

Bibliography

Actes Capitulaires du Chapitre de Notre-Dame de Chartres. G 298 (Registre), 1724-1726.

Andrews W, *Curious Church Customs.* London, 1898.

Andrews W, *Curious Church Gleanings.* Hull, 1896.

Archaeologia, vol LII.

Archaeologia, vol XXVI.

Ariès P, *Centuries of Childhood,* Paris, 1960. (English version Jonathan Cape, 1962.)

Arjona J S, *El teatro en Sevilla en los siglos.* Madrid, 1887.

Beletus, *de Divin. Offic.* cap 72 and cap 120.

Beziers M, *Histoire de Sommaire de la Ville de Bayeux.* Caen, 1773.

Bibl. Capit., MS 77, Consueta Barcinonensis seac. xiv-xv, fol.364. R B Donovan, "The Liturgical Drama in Medieval Spain", Toronto, 1958.

Bibl. Capit., Padua, MS S Ordin. Patavinense saec. xiii, fol 50^v- 53^v.

Bishop Grandisson's *Ordinale.*

Bled O, 'La Fête des Innocents dans l'église collégiale de Saint-Omer'. extract from *Bulletin historique* de la Société des Antiquaires de la Morinie, Saint Omer, 1887, quoted in E Hautcoeur, *Histoire de l'église collégiale et du chapitre de Saint-Pierre de Lille,* vol 2, Paris, 1896-1897.

Boemus Johannes, *Omnium Gentium Mores, Leges et Ritus.* Antwerp, 1562.

Boutiot T, *Histoire de la Ville de Troyes.* Troyes, vol III, 1873.

Boys W, *A History of Sandwich in Kent.* 1892.

Brand J, *Observations on Popular Antiquities.* (ed) Hazlitt, vol 1, London, 1805.

Calendar of Coroner's Rolls for the City of London A.D. 1300-1378. 1913.

Cattley (ed), *The Acts and Monuments of John Foxe.* vol VIII, London, 1839.

Chambers E K, *The Medieval Stage.* OUP, London, 1903.

Chérest A, 'Nouvelles Recherches sur la Fête des Innocents et la Fête des Fous'. *Bulletin de la Societé des Sciences de L'Yonne,* vol 7, 1853.

Clark J M, *The Abbey of St Gall as a Centre of Literature and Art.* Cambridge, 1926.

Cotman J S, *Architectural Antiquities of Normandy.* vol 1, London, 1822.

Crawford J P W, 'A Note on the Boy Bishop in Spain'. *Romanic Review,* vol 12, 1921.

Dahhaoui Y, 'Voyages d'un prélat festif'. *Revue historique* 3/2006 (N°639).

Denfile H, *Auctarium Chartularii Universitatis Parisiensis*, vol III.

Dickson T (ed), *Accounts of the Lord High Treasurer of Scotland*, vol 1.

Donovan R B, *The Liturgical Drama in Medieval Spain*. Toronto, 1958.

Du Cange C D, *Glossarium mediae et infimae Latinitatis conditum a Du Cangio, auctum a monachis Ordinis S. Benedicit, cum supplementis Carpenterii suisque digessit*. G A L Hensche,. Editio nova, aucta a L Favre, 10 vols, 1883-7, s. v. *Kalendae*.

Du Tilliot, *Memoires pour Servir a l'Histoire de la Fête des Foux*. Lausanne, 1751.

Dudley M R, 'Natalis Innocentum'. *The Church and Childhood,* D Wood (ed), Oxford, 1994.

Duffy E, *The Voices of Morebath*. Yale University Press, New Haven and London, 2001.

Dugdale W, *Monasticon Anglicanum*, vol III. London, 1846.

'Durham Account Rolls'. *The Surtees Society*, vols I-III.

Dürr F A, 'Commentatio Historica de Episcopo Puerorum'. *Thesaurus Iuris Ecclesiastica*, vol III, J Schmidt, 1772.

Edwards, K, *The English Secular Cathedrals in the Middle Ages*. The University Press, Manchester, 1949.

Erasmus, *Concio de Puero Jesu*. Ghent, 1513?

Erasmus, *On Civility in Children*.

Evelyn-White C H, 'The Boy Bishop (Episcopus Puerorum) of Mediaeval England Pt 1'. *Journal of the British Archaelogical Association,* vol XL, 1905.

Evelyn-White C H, 'The Boy Bishop (Episcopus Puerorum) of Mediaeval England Pt 2'. *Journal of the British Archaelogical Association,* vol XL. 1905.

Feilberg H F, *Jul.* Copenhagen, 1904, p. 254, quoted in C A Miles, *Christmas Ritual and Tradition,* vol 2, 1912.

Fletcher J M J, pp. 18-19, quoting Nicholls and Taylor, *Bristol Past and Present*, vol II.

Fletcher J M J, *The Boy Bishop at Salisbury and Elsewhere*. Salisbury, 1921.

Fleury E, *Cinquante Ans de l'Histoire du Chapitre de N-D de Laon*. Laon, 1875.

Gasquet F A, *Parish Life in Mediaeval England*. Methuen, London, 1907.

Gasquet F A, *The Old English Bible and Other Essays*. London, 1897.

Gasté A, *Les Drames Liturgiques de la Cathédrale de Rouen*. Evreux, 1893.

Gayley C M, *Plays of our Forefathers*. London, 1908.

Gregory J, *Episcopus Puerorum In Die Innocentium*. 1671.

Gregory J, *Episcopus Puerorum in Die Innocentium*. Opera Posthuma, London, 1649.

Grenier P N, *Introduction à l'Histoire général de la Province de Picardie*. 1856.

Hanawalt B A, *Growing Up in Medieval London*. OUP, Oxford, 1993.

Harris M, 'A Rough and Holy Liturgy: A Reassessment of the Feast of Fools'. Katja Gvozdeva and Werner Röcke (ed), *Risus Sacer – Risus Risible: Interaktionsfelder von Sakralität und Gelächter im kulturellen und historischen Wandel*, Peter Lang, Bern, 2009.

Hautcoeur E, *Histoire de l'église collégiale et du chapitre de Saint-Pierre de Lille*. 1897.

Hereford Breviary.

Hidé C, *Bulletin de la Societé Academique de Laon*. vol 13.

Hillebrand H N, *The Child Actors*. New York, 1964.

Hingeston-Randolph F C, *The Register of John de Grandisson, Bishop of Exeter*. Part III, London, 1899.

Hone W, *Ancient Mysteries Described*. London, 1823.

Huizinga J, *The Waning of the Middle Ages*. reprinted Penguin, 1987.

Iles P, *The Boy Bishop Ceremony*. R J L Smith and Associates, Much Wenlock, 1992.

Jones and Dayman, *Sarum Statutes*.

Laborde, *Les Ducs de Borgogne*. vol II, Paris, 1851.

Leach A F, 'The Schoolboys' Feast'. *The Fortnightly Review*, vol 14, 1896.

Louth Churchwardens' Accounts, quoted in E Howlett, 'Boy Bishops', W Andrews (ed),*Curious Church Gleanings*, Hull, 1896.

Lucian, *Saturnalia*

Lupton J H (ed), *Sermon on the Chylde Jesus*. London, 1901.

Lysons D, *The Environs of London*. vol 1, London, 1792.

Martene E, *De Antiquis Ecclesiae Ritibus*, vol III, (Liber IV Caput XIII).

Martindale A, 'The Child in the Picture: a Medieval Perspective'. D Wood (ed) *The Church and Childhood*, Oxford, 1994.

Meller W C, *The Boy Bishop and Other Essays*. London, 1923.

Miles C A, *Christmas in Ritual and Tradition*. T Fisher Unwin, 1912.

Millard J E, *Historical Notices of the Office of Choristers*. 1848.

'Missale ad Usum Insignis Ecclesiae Eboracensis'. *The Surtees Society*, vol 1, Durham, 1874.

Morse-Boycott D, *The Boy Bishop Book*. 1946. This book seems to have been privately printed and distributed but is available in the British Library, shelfmark 3478.bb.59. I can find no other source for this account.

Mortimer I, *The Time Traveller's Guide to Medieval England*. The Bodley Head, London, 2008.

Nicholls J G (ed), *The Diary of Henry Machyn from 1550 AD to 1563 AD*. London, 1848.

Ordo IX Lugdunensis.

Nicholls J F and Taylor J, *Bristol Past and Present*, vols I-III, J W Arrowsmith, Bristol, 1881-1882

Nicholson S H, *Peter: The Adventures of a Chorister*. 1945

Paris, BnF, ms. lat. 17123. p 357, quoted in Dahhaoui Y, 'Voyages d'un prélat festif', *Revue historique* 3/2006 (N°639).

Pearsall C E (ed), *The History and Genealogy of the Pearsall Family in England and America*. San Francisco, 1928.

Percy T (ed), *The Regulations and Establishment of the Household of Algernon Percy the fifth Earl of Northumberland*, 1827.

Pertz G H, *Monumenta Germaniae Historica Scriptorum*, vol XXIII. Hanover, 1874.

Petit de Julleville L, *Histoire du théâtre en France*. Paris, 1886.

Picard A, *Ordinaire et coutumier de l'Eglise Cathédrale de Bayuex*. Paris, 1902.

Pilot de Thorey J J A, *Usages, Fêtes, et Coutumes existent ou ayant existé en Dauphiné*. vol 1, Grenoble, 1884.

Planché J R, 'On the Sepulchral Effigies in Salisbury Cathedral'. *Journal of the British Archaeological Society*, vol 15, 1854.

Poinsignon M, *Histoire Générale de la Champagne et de la Brie*. vol II, 2nd ed., Chalons-sur- Marne, 1897, pp. 29-30.

Pynson R, *Processionale ad Usum Sarum*, 1502.

Raine J, 'Fabric Rolls of York Minster'. *The Surtees Society*, vol XXV, 1859.

Registr. Archiv. Eccles. Ebor. MSS.

Reynolds H E (ed), *Wells Cathedral: Its Foundation, Constitutional History, and Statutes*. Leeds.

Rigollot M J, *Monnaies inconnues des Evêques des Innocens, des Fous, et quelque autres Associations singulières du meme Temps*. 1837.

Rimbault E F, 'Two Sermons Preached by the Boy Bishop'. *The Camden Miscellany*, vol VII, 1875.

Robertson D H, *Sarum Close*. London, 1938.

Rock D, *The Church of Our Fathers*. vol III, London, 1852.

Shergold N D, *A History of the Spanish Stage*. Oxford, 1967.

Sparrow Simpson W (ed), *Registrum Statutorum et Consuetudinum Ecclesiae Cathedralis Sancti Pauli Londiniensis*. London, 1873.

Specht F A, *Geschichte des Unterrichtswens in Deutschland*. 1967 (reprinted).

Statutes of Bishop Grandisson (1337). quoted in T Warton, *The History of English Poetry*, London, 1840, vol II.

Strype J, *Ecclesiatical Memorials*. London, 1823

Stuart J (ed), *Extracts from the Council Register of the Burgh of Aberdeen*, vol I.

Symond's Lesson for All Manner of Children (15th century poem).

Taylor J, 'Prophetic "Play" and Symbolist Plot in the Beauvais *Daniel*'. C Davidson, C J Gianakaris and J H Stroupe, (eds), *The Drama of the Middle Ages: Comparative and Critical Essays*, AMS Press, New York, 1982.

The Statute Book (York) YM M1/1/b.

The Boy Bishop – A Ballad of Old Halifax. Halifax, 1877.

Thiers J B, *Traité de Jeux et des Divertissenens*. Paris, 1686.

Tille A, *Die Geschichte der deutschen Weihnacht*. Leipsic, 1893.

Timperely C H, *A Dictionary of Printers and Printing*, London . 1839.

Villetard H (ed), *Office de Pierre de Corbeil (Office de la Circoncision) improprement appelé "Office des Fous"*. Paris: Alphonse Picard, 1907.

Warton T, Hazlitt (ed), *The History of English Poetry*, vol II. 1871.

Warton T, *The History of English Poetry*, vol III. London, 1840.

Wilkins's *Concilia*. quoted in E F Rimbault.

Wordsworth C (ed), *Ceremonies and Processions of the Cathedral Church of Salisbury*. Cambridge, 1901.

Young K, *The Drama of the Medieval Church*. vol II, Oxford, 1933.